ALSO BY GENE WEINGARTEN

The Hypochondriac's Guide to Life. And Death.

ALSO BY GINA BARRECA

Babes in Boyland:
A Personal History of Co-Education in the Ivy Leagues

Don't Tell Mama!:
The Penguin Book of Italian American Writing, editor

Too Much of a Good Thing Is Wonderful

The Signet Book of American Humor, editor

The Penguin Book of Women's Humor, editor

Perfect Husbands and Other Fairy Tales:
Demystifying Marriage, Men and Romance

"Untamed and Unabashed":
Essays on Women and Comedy in Literature

They Used to Call Me Snow White . . . but I Drifted:
Women's Strategic Use of Humor

I'M
WITH
STUPID

One Man. One Woman.
10,000 Years of Misunderstanding
Between the Sexes Cleared Right Up

Gene
Weingarten & ## Gina
Barreca

ILLUSTRATIONS BY RICHARD THOMPSON

SIMON & SCHUSTER PAPERBACKS
NEW YORK LONDON TORONTO SYDNEY

SIMON & SCHUSTER PAPERBACKS
Rockefeller Center
1230 Avenue of the Americas
New York, NY 10020

First Simon & Schuster paperback edition 2006

SIMON & SCHUSTER and colophon are registered trademarks
of Simon & Schuster, Inc.

For information regarding special discounts for bulk purchases,
please contact Simon & Schuster Special Sales at 1-800-456-6798
or business@simonandschuster.com

Book design by Ellen R. Sasahara
Illustrations copyright © 2004 by Richard Thompson

Manufactured in the United States of America

10   9   8   7   6   5   4   3   2   1

The Library of Congress has cataloged the hardcover edition as follows:

Weingarten, Gene.
I'm with stupid : One man. One woman. 10,000 years of misunderstanding between
the sexes cleared right up / Gene Weingarten & Gina Barreca.
p.   cm.
1. Sex differences (Psychology)—Humor. 2. Sex role—Humor. I. Title: I'm with
stupid, one man. one woman. ten thousand years of misunderstanding between
the sexes cleared right up. II. Barreca, Regina. III. Title.
PN6231.S542W45 2004
818'.5407—dc22   2003066784

ISBN-13: 978-0-7432-4420-6

ISBN-13: 978-0-7432-7888-1 (Pbk.)

GENE WEINGARTEN:

To Molly, Dan, and their mother, the dog food lady.

GINA BARRECA:

For my husband, Michael Meyer, whom I adore.

ACKNOWLEDGMENTS

GENE WEINGARTEN

Several chapters in this book were adapted from material that first appeared in my column in *The Washington Post Magazine*. They are included here by permission of Donald Graham—chairman and CEO of The Washington Post Company—to whom I am indebted not only for this kindness but for piloting a newspaper of such stature and integrity that the work of all *Post* writers carries weight and influence. I hope this book does not betray that trust, but to the extent that it does, it is Gina's fault.

At the *Post,* I thank editors John Cotter, Brian Miller, and Bill O'Brian, and Mary Lou White, the Sam Spade of newspaper librarians. If Mary Lou can't find you, you do not exist. Also, David Von Drehle for his wisdom, Tamara Jones and Hank Stuever for their generosity in letting me pirate some of their funny observations, and Joel Achenbach for simply letting me watch him cope with life. It's a hoot.

I am grateful to our publisher, David Rosenthal, for wanting this book, and for coming up with the perfect title in three minutes after Gina and I spent three months failing to do so. Our editor, Amanda Murray, provided valuable guidance throughout.

The magnificent eccentricity of our agent, Al Hart, inspired half a chapter.

I thank my friend Dave Barry, who provided an important impetus at a critical time. Early on, when Simon and Schuster expressed an interest in this book but several of my other friends urged me in a different direction, it was Dave who put everything in perspective. "How much are you being offered to write the book?" he asked. I told him. "Good. Now how much are your friends offering you *not* to write the book?" Gina and I signed the next day.

Pat Myers, the world's funniest copy editor, has managed to wrestle the words into shape so as to mask my illiteracy and intellectual lassitude; her own humor surfaces in the text time and again. And finally, I thank my friend and boss Tom Shroder, the editor at the *Post* who has refereed the Gene-Gina wars from the start. Tom is belligerent, arrogant, insufferably intolerant of all views not his own, and in general a sockdologizing old poop who is of no value whatsoever except for being the best humor editor alive.

GINA BARRECA

Of course the first person who must be thanked immediately and from the heart is the person without whom this book would not exist: my co-author, Gene Weingarten. Can you even *imagine* somebody leaving his co-author out of the acknowledgments? No, because that level of insensitivity and self-absorption does not exist on this planet, at least outside the male brain. So, Gene, you come first. Naturally.

Naturally, too, I thank everybody Gene thanks, too. Except I thank them *more*. And sincerely. I also want to thank Click and Clack from NPR's *Car Talk* for reading a couple of the columns on their show. It made my relatives think I finally made use of my education.

I also thank the following tribe from Connecticut—many from UConn, where I teach—and also New York: Mara Reisman, Barbara Campbell, Margaret Mitchell, Nancy Lager and Tim Taylor, Pam Katz, Bonnie Januszewski, Rose Quiello, Amy Bloom and Joy Johannason, and Fleur and Jerry Lawrence. They read and listened and laughed and gave me my best lines.

Heidi Rockefeller deserves her own line because nearly every Friday afternoon when Gene and I were on the phone yelling at each other, groaning, Heidi—while organizing the papers on my desk or shooing the cats off my printer—would come up with the perfect solution or idea.

Thanks to Tim and Matthew, my two relentlessly brilliant stepsons, for their encouragement and the high standards they apply to humor. Thanks to my father, Hugo, and my brother, Hugo, and my nephew, Hugo—and to my sister-in-law, Wendy, who has a terrific laugh, one she passed on to amazing Anne and fabulous Laura. They made a great cheering section.

And finally, of course, because it cannot possibly be overstated, I thank Gene.

CONTENTS

The Phlogiston Theory of Sexual Relations, or Why This Book Will Change Your Life

GENE: At this very moment you may well be standing in a bookstore, trying to decide whether to purchase this book—which, you deduce from the cover, involves differences between men and women. And because you are an intelligently skeptical person, you are thinking: Why should I spend my good money on a book that is rehashing the most tired subject on earth, a subject long ago chewed into an amorphous goo, like the food in your mouth the instant before you swallow it, a slimy succotash barely distinguishable from vomit?

Come to think of it, wouldn't that be a great diet? You could eat as much food as you wanted, and absolutely any food you wanted, except that just before every swallow you would have to look in the mirror and stare at the slop on your tongue for five seconds. I'll bet that would—

GINA: Stop.

GENE: What?

GINA: That's disgusting. We can't start this book in that disgusting, immature way.

GENE: It's a diet tip! Women *love* diet tips!

GINA: Kindly do not tell me what women love.

GENE: Diet books fly off the shelves.

GINA: One, that's not a diet, it's an eating disorder. Two, this is not a diet book.

GENE: It could be. We haven't written it yet.

GINA: It's supposed to be about men and women, and humor.

GENE: Well, I'm simply trying to explain how clichéd and lifeless this subject matter is. How it has been explored and debated ad nauseam from Aristotle to Woolf, diluted into an insipid, gelatinous soup by communication experts and gender experts, and then salted with poison by every adenoidal comic who ever stood in front of a brick wall with a microphone and an inflated sense of self. I was merely trying to communicate how difficult it is to infuse this subject with anything even resembling originality or insight, and how only a fool or an egotist would attempt it.

GINA: We are writing an introduction. To the book. To get people to buy it.

GENE: Yes, we are

GINA: Do you think, perhaps, we might consider another approach?

GENE:

GINA: Not that there's anything wrong with your approach.

GENE: Are you patronizing me?

GINA: I would not attempt to patronize someone as smart and funny and strong and manly as you are. I was just thinking we might begin in a less overtly self-destructive fashion. For example, we might explain how you and I met.

GENE: With women, it's always about relationships.

GINA: Tell them how we met, or I will. In my version, you look very bad.

GENE: I write a humor column for *The Washington Post Magazine*. This means that every single week I have to come up with a funny idea, which means that occasionally I am reduced to reading my office mail, which pretty much consists of (1) semiliterate persons calling me names or (2) public relations agents trying to sell me a can't-miss humorous story idea, such as the wonderfulness of a client's new line of decorative pillows. One day, I came across a press release about a new book by Gina Barreca, a University of Connecticut English professor who was identified as an expert in "humor and feminism."

Two things immediately occurred to me. The first was that a person being an expert in humor and feminism was like a person being an expert in oysters and accordions; I concluded that here was a terrific opportunity to plumb important sociological verities by humiliating some hapless, unfunny girl academic. The second thing that occurred to me was that my name was Gene, and hers was Gina, and that this was providential.

GINA: This is the part I hate. The gimmicky part.

GENE: You don't hate the "hapless, unfunny girl academic" part?

GINA: No. I am not a hapless, unfunny girl academic. You discovered that, didn't you?

GENE: Yes, I did.

GINA: Tell them how you discovered that.

GENE: In a minute.

GINA: Tell them now, or *I* will. In my version, you look very bad.

GENE: We had a humor contest in my column. And the readers voted.

GINA: And who won?

GENE: Gina.

GINA: Thank you. That was magnanimous.

GENE: Anyway, we kept doing columns, and we had this nifty name shtick going, and after a while I wandered over to Simon and Schuster and landed us a book contract.

GINA: The names are irrelevant. This isn't a book because of some stupid gimmick. This is a book because we will reveal intriguing truths about human relationships in a funny and engaging manner. We'd be writing this even if I were Rhonda and you were Norman.

GENE: Norman and Rhonda?

GINA: Rhonda and Norman. Absolutely. Just as good.

DAVID ROSENTHAL: No, it's not.

GINA: Who are you?

GENE: He's our publisher at Simon and Schuster. I invited him. David, this is Gina.

DAVID: Charmed, I'm sure.

GENE: Rhonda and Norman. Contract or no?

DAVID: You walk in as Rhonda and Norman, I laugh you out the door. The gimmick is everything. You guys could be transcribing the Beijing phone book, for all it matters.

GENE: Thanks, David. Appreciate your stopping by.

DAVID: Glad to oblige.

GINA:

GENE: Just so we understand things.

GINA: We understand nothing. Our editor, Amanda Murray, told me she thinks this is going to rest on the strength of our ideas, the universality of our themes, and the chemistry that'll develop between us.

GENE: May I point out that Amanda's opinion, while certainly elegant, is also irrelevant? David is her boss.

GINA: Imagine my surprise. The American book industry employs thirty thousand women and six men. Guess who are the publishers?

GENE: Can we postpone the grating neofeminist tirades for one chapter at least?

GINA: People need to know there will be interesting, provocative material in this book.

GENE: Well, there'll be smutty parts.

GINA: Yes, but they'll be thematically justified. They will not be prurient.

GENE: Whatever.

GINA: We also should probably apologize for generalizing.

GENE: We haven't written anything yet. You want to apologize already?

GINA: A book like this is bound to contain some unfortunate, broad-brush assertions about human behavior. We'll declare that "men do this" and "women do that" without acknowledging the obvious fact that there are exceptions. We need to ask the reader to understand that the need to be funny requires conciseness, and conciseness requires shortcuts. We have to assure them that we will make every effort to avoid unnecessary or hurtful generalizations, and we have to hope they take no offense when we can't.

GENE: Fat chance. All readers are oversensitive, hypercritical meatheads.

GINA:

GENE: That was a joke. It's a *humor* book. We're allowed to make jokes.

GINA: We also need to point out that we're dealing only with heterosexual relationships. We cannot presume to speak for gay people, or speculate on how gay men and women relate.

GENE: You mean how gay men relate to gay women?

GINA: Right. Or gay men to straight women.

GENE: How about straight men to gay women?

GINA: What difference does it make? We're not going there, period. Okay?

GENE: Okay.

GINA: Okay.

GENE: How about straight women to preoperative transgendered men?

GINA:

GENE: What?

GINA: I think I also want to make it emphatically clear that we are not an item. You and I.

GENE: I don't mind if people think that.

GINA: I do.

GENE: Okay, we're not an item. In fact, Gina and I have never met in person—and we don't intend to. We correspond entirely by telephone and e-mail. Actually, Rosenthal wants it that way.

GINA: He does?

GENE: Yes. He wants us to meet for the first time on the book tour, to generate "buzz."

GINA: Gimme a break.

GENE: It's true. The publishing industry thrives on buzz.

GINA: Does Simon and Schuster make Bob Woodward manufacture his own buzz?

GENE: I don't think he has to. Bob's buzz is natural. He travels with it, like a horsefly.

GINA: The whole arrangement seems manipulative. I'm not sure I'm comfortable with it.

GENE: You were comfortable with not meeting me before you knew you weren't allowed to meet me. Now you want to meet me?

GINA: I want to make it clear that it is in my power to meet you should I desire to do so. This is entirely at my discretion. We are centuries removed from chastity belts and chaperones and other measures engineered by men to restrict the freedom of women to go where they want and do as they wish.

GENE: Fine. Do you want to meet?

GINA: No.

GENE: Okay, then.

GINA: And since we're on the subject of the depths to which publishers will sink, I think we need to explain that this book is not going to be like John Gray's *Men Are from Mars, Women Are from Venus*. That was condescending. And chauvinistic. And dry.

GENE: It also sold sixteen squintillion copies. It's been translated into 740 languages, including several that are entirely clicks and diphthongs. There's probably a version printed in Wingdings, like this: ⌧&✦⽘⟐⳾⳾●✦⟐

GINA: Well, that's my point. The subject is inherently interesting.

GENE: Yes, but I suspect that our Mars and Venus will breach their orbits and collide in a screaming fireball from hell.

GINA: No problem. I like fireworks. What I'm saying is that this subject doesn't have to be delivered in some humorless, pedantic fashion by a man.

GENE: It's the *man's* fault?

GINA: It usually is.

GENE: How about *The Rules,* by Ellen Fein and Sherrie Schneider—that runaway best-seller about how women need to bat their eyes and coyly withhold sex to catch a husband. Have you read it?

GINA: I have.

GENE: Did you or did you not want to puke?

GINA: I did.

GENE: So what's your point?

GINA: My point is, we're not a man *or* a woman. We're both.

GENE: We're a hermaphrodite? We have frighteningly ambiguous genitalia?

GINA: I prefer to think of us as Tiresias.

GENE: Who?

GINA: The blind prophet from Greek mythology. He lived first as a man and then as a woman. This book will be the Tiresias of humor—a single sentience, privy to the dark secrets of both sexes.

GENE: Wow.

GINA: I have a Ph.D.

GENE: I dropped out of college to join a street gang in the South Bronx.

GINA: I know. I'm slumming.

GENE: So we'll go chapter by chapter, visiting subjects about which men and women disagree.

GINA: Are there any subjects about which men and women do not disagree?

GENE: The reprehensibility of Hitler. We won't visit that.

GINA: Fine.

GENE: On all other matters, we'll basically be beating each other up.

GINA: We will not. That is a barbarous expression only a man would use. We will engage in a spirited and sometimes contentious exchange of views. The important point is that we're not going to be writing familiar pablum handed down ex cathedra by one gender or the other. What we produce will be an entirely new substance, formed by the combustion of both.

GENE: Okay. I'm with you.

GINA: So, what should we call it?

GENE: The book?

GINA: The substance.

GENE: Does it have to have a name?

GINA: It would give us greater standing as contemporary social scientists.

GENE: You're good.

GINA: I'm an academic. This is what we do.

GENE: Well, if what we're writing is the product of combustion, and if we're scientists, let's call it phlogiston.

GINA: What's that?

GENE: A product of combustion, according to a highly regarded nineteenth-century scientific theory.

GINA: I never heard of it.

GENE: Of course not. It was wrong. Ludicrously wrong. But people believed it for more than a hundred years. You see where I'm going here?

GINA: No.

GENE: If we're scientists, we don't have to be right. We just have to sound sure of ourselves. Being wrong is a hallowed part of the scientific process. For example, Pluto isn't even a real *planet.* We know that now, but the guy who discovered it died as the Magellan of the cosmos.

As scientists, we can tell people whatever we want. We can tell them that if they don't buy this book, they'll never get laid again.

GINA: That won't work for women. Women can always get laid, and we know it. Besides, women want something more meaningful. We want spiritual and emotional fulfillment.

GENE: Swell. We'll promise them that. Phlogiston is a miracle substance.

GINA: What color is it?

GENE: Ha ha.

GINA: No, really. We need to agree on this.

GENE: You want to know the color of a substance that does not exist that stands as a metaphor for the texture of a relationship that has not yet developed in a book that is not yet written?

GINA: Yes.

GENE:

GINA: We have to resolve this before I agree.

GENE: It's pink.

GINA: Splendid.

GENE: Happy now?

GINA: Quite.

GENE: I don't think I like the way this is starting out.

GINA: I do.

1

Sex and the Single Cell:
How It All Began

GINA: Why are there two sexes? Why not just one, or three?

GENE: I'd say the answer depends on your system of beliefs. According to Judeo-Christian tradition, for example, it was a decision by God. God created Adam in His own image, and then as an afterthought fashioned Eve from Adam's rib to be his, and I quote, "helpmeat."

GINA: Help*meet*.

GENE: Translation from ancient Hebrew is imprecise. The point is clear. To the rigorous theologian, the central and inescapable conclusion of this biblical allegory is: God has a penis.

To repeat, documentary evidence establishes persuasively that the deity is a man——with a prominent Adam's apple, a disdain for romantic comedies, and an almost religious appreciation of televised sporting events.

Still there, Gina?

GINA: I am.

GENE: Why aren't you objecting?

GINA: You haven't said anything I disagree with.

GENE: You concede that God is male?

GINA: Yes.

GENE: I thought feminists would disagree.

GINA: Feminists do not ignore the plainly evident just because it happens to be annoying or inconvenient. God creates the world in all its splendor and plenty—poof, a cornucopia of all things good and sweet—and then proceeds, as His first administrative act, to place everyone on a diet? A *food restriction*? This is a male God. In a female God's paradise, you eat what you want. Plus, there would be no river named "Pishon."

GENE: Pishon?

GINA: According to Genesis, that's the name of the first river. Pishon is a name a guy God comes up with. It takes Him four seconds. He's busy, He's got a lot on his plate, He doesn't care. "Okay, lessee, we got a river here, we'll call it, I dunno, Pishon. Next!" A woman God names the first river something like Sweetbriar Estuary.

GENE: You've given some thought to this.

GINA: I haven't wanted to. It's unavoidable. Advance a few dozen millennia, and you find God looking for a woman to bear the baby Jesus. His first criterion is that she is a virgin. Listen, there is not a woman alive who gives a crap about who is a virgin and who is not. This is an entirely male preoccupation. So, yeah, God is a man. That pretty much explains endometriosis.

GENE: You sound bitter.

GINA: No, just resigned. A guy God answers a lot of questions, including why women are still earning seventy-five cents on the male dollar. Anyway, it's not my favorite creation scenario. You got another one?

GENE: That would be that humans evolved over millions of years from single-cell organisms. At some point during this process, in the primordial ooze of the early Paleozoic period, two sexes developed as an adaptation to better shuffle the gene pool and make the various species more developmentally supple. Thus, complex organisms became more resistant to the onslaught of opportunistic disease and more likely to evolve. I think we can all agree this is fine as far as it goes, but it still does not explain why women cannot seem to parallel-park a car without smooshing one tire against the curb.

GINA: Actually, you raise an important question.

GENE: I know. We're talking about the tragedy of needless sidewall damage.

GINA: You asked it in a typically hostile and adolescent fashion, but the question is valid: Why are obviously necessary and explicable anatomical sexual differences accompanied by seemingly unnecessary and inexplicable gender-based behavioral differences?

GENE: Right. Like tire smooshing. Or the color thing.

GINA: The color thing?

GENE: You know, the fact that eggplants are purple.

GINA: Eggplants are not purple. Eggplants are eggplant. Or aubergine. Or indigo-violet.

GENE: This is precisely my point. The color thing.

GINA: As it happens, gender differences in color sensitivity can be explained. It's Darwinian. In most species, the male is more colorful—so, in courting, the female needs to be able to distinguish a teal neck ruff from a turquoise one from one that is yet another subtle shade that would have no meaning to you, a shlumpy male. But it does not explain the many other areas in which men and women seem to diverge in outlook, proclivities, priorities, emotions, and so on. In short, the mysteries of gender.

GENE: Dames—who can figure 'em?

GINA: And right there we can observe another behavioral difference. Women care about behavioral differences, and men do not. Women are fascinated by them, obsessed by them, plagued by them, intent upon analyzing them so as to better adapt to them. Men are content to throw up their hands and say, "Dames—who can figure 'em?"

GENE: I object to that. Men notice the behavioral differences, and we care about them.

GINA: Only to the extent that they can interfere with your ability to obtain sex.

GENE: Well, that's a very sincere form of caring!

GINA: Honestly, have you ever taken any time at all to reflect about how women behave?

GENE: Yes, I have.

GINA: Share your reflections.

GENE: I have never understood why women fret about visible panty lines and waste so much time trying to hide them. Hasn't anyone informed them that men *love* visible panty lines? This behavior is a total mystery.

GINA: I'm speechless. I just don't know what to say.

GENE: You could compliment me on my powers of observation and analysis.

GINA: Does the panty paradox exhaust your arsenal of philosophical inquiry?

GENE: I can't think of anything else at the moment.

GINA: I see.

GENE: You've got more questions?

GINA: I can think of one or two.

GENE: Shoot.

GINA: Why do women feel guilty about everything and men nothing? Why, when you ask a man how he's feeling, does he survey himself and think, "I'm not cold, I'm not hungry, I'm okay," and when you ask a woman how she's feeling, she begins with "I've been insecure lately, does it show? Is that why you're asking? I've got issues, but I'm working on them. . . ." and so forth?

Why do women care about the color of sheets and towels? Why do men care about the way maps are folded? Why do women have long fingernails that they are encouraged to make into objects of art, while men with long fingernails look like Nosferatu? Why are men turned on by the thought of two women having sex but the idea of two men having sex doesn't do a thing for a woman? Why don't men stock up on greeting cards for future occasions?

Why do women take care of the photographs in every household while men take most of the pictures? Why do men hate pink? Why do only women like music boxes? Why do men like excavating machines? Why are men so frightened of menses that any mention of it—incidental or tactical—will send them scurrying away? And is this what is really meant by "feminine protection"?

Would you rather have your beloved have sex with somebody else who is only vaguely important emotionally or fall in love with—but never touch—the other person? I know. Well, women feel the other way. Why is that? And why don't men ask questions like this?

Why don't men like older women (meaning older than me)

when women like older men? Why are men frightened by big women? Why are men's urinals so public? Why do women, but not men, leave eleven-minute messages on answering machines? Why do men like helicopters? Why do women save nice paper bags from fancy stores?

Why do men have such trouble getting along with their fathers and why do they think it's such a big honking sad deal that every piece of "important" literature in some way reflects this titanic struggle? Why don't men ever admit they feel cold?

Why do men carry four thousand dollars' worth of loose change in their pockets at all times but always present a twenty to the cashier? Why do women like miniatures? Why it is considered part of the woman's job to make sure her family is neither constipated nor afflicted with diarrhea? Why do women buy books about men's inner turmoil but men do not buy books about women's inner turmoil?

Why is the theme song for women's relationships "Will You Still Love Me Tomorrow?" whereas for men it is "We've Got Tonight, Why Don't You Stay?" Why do men want to have sex with women they would never introduce to anybody they actually knew because it would be too embarrassing? Why do women want to introduce some guy they are sleeping with to everybody they have ever met?

Why do men like kissing for a long time at the beginning of a romance but then you have to make an appointment with them to get kissed for more than five seconds after you've been in said relationship for a couple of years? Would you rather be in bed with a woman who could make you laugh or a woman with a twenty-four-inch waist? Do you think a woman would rather be in bed with a man who could make her laugh or one hung like a sixteen-ounce can of Bud? Are you sure? I didn't think so. Why is that?

GENE: You are irritating, do you know that?

GINA: I am interesting and educational.

GENE: That was extremely passive-aggressive.

GINA: It was not.

GENE: Why are women so passive-aggressive?

GINA: Good for you. You found another question.

2

It's Not Merely Amusing—
It's Historical

GENE: Men are, and have always been, the principal architects of history.

GINA: Agreed. But—

GENE: No, allow me. Women's comparative insignificance as major players in the advance of civilization is the result of their virtual enslavement over thousands of years by the rigors and restrictions of their biological responsibilities. Though requiring enormous fortitude and emotional strength, this role remained subordinate, a condition perpetuated by men, who actively prevented women from achieving even a semblance of economic independence, political enfranchisement, social parity, or even literacy.

GINA: Agreed.

GENE: Because of this palpable disadvantage—undiminished until very recently by advances in contraception, universal education, and other fruits of nascent feminist social movements—only a bigot or an ignoramus could survey the breadth of civilization and conclude that the female sex has shown itself innately deficient in the capacity to lead, or to create, or to pioneer in important fields of endeavor. The inescapable fact is that, until modern times, women simply haven't been given the chance.

GINA:

GENE: What?

GINA: I am waiting for your uncontrollable spasm of misogyny.

GENE: I just want to be fair about this.

GINA: Uh-huh.

GENE: Really.

GINA: Why don't you just let it out? It'll be good for you. Clear the air.

GENE: Aristotle Beethoven Confucius Da Vinci Einstein Franklin Gandhi Hippocrates Ibsen Jesus Kafka Lincoln Mandela Newton Orwell Pericles Quintilian Roosevelt Saladin Tolstoy Utrillo Van Gogh Washington Xavier Yeats Zoroaster.

GINA: Feel better now?

GENE: Yes. Thank you.

GINA: Pol Pot, Vlad the Impaler, Vanilla Ice . . .

GENE: No need to go there. We are at a rare point of agreement. History belongs to men. Eventually it will not.

GINA: We are not at a rare point of agreement. We are at a predictable point of disagreement. You are defining history as a relentless march of progress. I define it as an appalling parade of debauchery and oppression perpetrated by bloodthirsty lunatics with penises, interrupted by the very occasional humanitarian achievement. History would have been entirely different, and better, if women had been the dominant sex.

Unfortunately, the die was cast from the earliest stirrings of civilization. The women were squatting in caves and yurts, conceiving babies, birthing babies, nurturing babies. They turned to the men and said, "We're busy in here perpetuating the species—go, get out of the house. Find something to do. Make history." So the men went out and got into trouble.

GENE: And then?

GINA: And then nothing. That's history. History is men bumbling out of the house and getting into trouble. History, as recorded by men, has traditionally been a chronology of wars. This does not occur in a matriarchal society. In a matriarchal society, there is no war.

GENE: You think a world designed by women is a paradise?

GINA: I didn't say that. I said there would be no war. I did not say there would be no stresses. There would be bitchiness. There would be crankiness. There would be sarcastic remarks. My point is that hostilities between nations would be entirely different things. You would hurt their feelings.

GENE: That's it?

GINA: That's plenty. It might even escalate, because that is the nature of the human species. In time, regrettably, societies would develop weapons of mass hurt feelings. These would be cruel, I do not deny it. Like, you would make sweeping public statements about the children in the other country: "Your children are ugly and have bad table manners." Then you would feel terrible, and you'd talk about it. There'd be a lot of communication. In a matriarchal society, the telephone would have been invented very, very early, right after the wheel. But my key point is, no wars.

GENE: There would be no territorial disputes? No one would want anyone else's land?

GINA: Why would you want someone else's land? You can visit. If you own it, it's just more to clean.

GENE: Slavery?

GINA: No. It's true that women have a weakness for servants. But they go to great lengths to secure the admiration and respect of their servants. A woman will clean her house before the cleaning lady comes so that the cleaning lady won't think she's a slob.

Actually, in a world run by women, women would be each other's slaves. They would clean each other's houses. Women love to do that. You're much better at another woman's house than your own. Give a woman a shot at another woman's closet, for example, and she'll sweep that sucker clean of anything that wouldn't look good on her friend or that's been out of style for sixteen years and unwisely kept for sentimental purposes. It is very gratifying. That's why women all gather in the kitchen and do the dishes together.

So, no slavery per se. Reciprocal servitude. An excellent arrangement.

GENE: Religious persecution?

GINA: No. There might have been a Catholic Church, for example, but it would not have had a hierarchy. Women do not like hierarchies. So there would have been no burnings and lynchings and autos-da-fé. No Crusades. The church would have been mainly for tapestries.

I am not saying a matriarchal society would be perfect. I am saying it would be vastly more peaceful. No society run by women is sending its sons and daughters to be slaughtered by the sons and daughters of another society run by women. Control of the spice trade is not a reason for genocide. Women do not go to war over nutmeg.

Basically, women historians would not have been reduced to defining pivotal moments in history by battlefield events. Chapter 12 would not be "The Defeat of the Spanish Armada." That would not be the sort of thing to usher in a new era. Eras would be defined by collective realizations about the nature of harmony, goodwill, and better living through cooperation. Chapter 12 might be "When We Learned That if You Wash Your Hands You Get Sick Less." *That* would start an era.

Cooking with Garlic, another era. An important pivot of history would be the Discovery That Taking Turns Works Well in Most Situations. A major historical figure from the 1200s would be named something like Phoebe the Nice. She would have an assistant, Francine the Amusing. We would currently be in the Era of Good Feeling Because of Epidural Injections.

GENE: Hard to argue with this sort of logic.

GINA: It certainly seems evident to me.

GENE: So I guess if we examine the grand sweep of history, wherever we *do* find women who rose to positions of power and prestige, we will discover rare pockets of benevolence dotting the savage landscape of a male-dominated world. Take Queen Isabella of Spain, who is mostly known for spreading cheer among orphans, building vast libraries to educate the rabble, and sprinkling the countryside with parks and flower gardens, to the delight of millions . . . .

Oh, no, wait. My mistake. Isabella was the one who is mostly known for personally starting the Spanish Inquisition by instructing Torquemada to crush people into beanbags. She was certainly a feminist, though. She made sure her female descendants had every opportunity to rise to power. Her granddaughter was Queen

Mary I of England. That's the one they called "Mary the Positively Adorable."

Oh, hold it. That's not right. They called her Bloody Mary. She must have invented the Bloody Mary mix.

GINA: Having fun?

GENE: Hey, looky here. It turns out Mary earned the name by personally ordering hundreds of heretics burned to death from the feet up! Sometimes they'd have packets of gunpowder attached to their limbs so that prior to dying, they would get to watch their feet or arms blown off.

Elizabeth I, the paragon of all female monarchs, killed three cousins who threatened her power. And then there are the early years of the medieval Frankish Empire, in which several women rose to absolute power and distinguished themselves in entertaining ways. In the sixth century, Fredegund terrorized Paris for twenty years in a bloodthirsty exterminocracy considered one of the most sadistic and monstrous reigns in all of history. She made Caligula look like Eleanor Roosevelt. In time, Fredegund wrested the throne of Nuestria from her sister-in-law, the nearly equally savage Brunhilde, and gave it to her thirteen-year-old son, Chlotar. Chlotar thanked his mom by having Brunhilde dragged to death by a wild horse.

GINA: These were women who were born into male roles. This was the behavior expected of them, and they were accommodating. They became the sons their fathers couldn't have. When a woman acts like a man, she becomes a prick. She turns into Sigourney Weaver in *Working Girl*—the Phallic Princess.

GENE: I will just allow that feeble response to marinate in the skeptical silence of our readers of both sexes.

GINA: It's absolutely true.

GENE: Besides, let's examine your panacea for a moment. In your matriarchal society, how did women get to become the dominant sex?

GINA: Men would have been the ones to carry the babies and nurture them. So, from the beginning of time, men would have played a subservient role.

GENE: Problem: Men as we know them would not have sex if it meant carrying babies. Out of the question. One generation, max, and the species dies out due to precoital headaches.

GINA: Well, they wouldn't be men as we know them. They'd have uteruses and breasts and the instinct to nurture.

GENE: And women would have penises and scratch their balls.

GINA: Hmm.

GENE: You see where I'm going here.

GINA: I do. Well, my panacea works better in a world entirely composed of women, which, come to think of it, has now technologically become possible.

GENE: Huh?

GINA: Cloning. It could replace intercourse as the prime source of offspring. You can clone a baby of either sex, but it requires a woman to carry the baby to term. So you couldn't have a world of only men, but you could have a world of only women. Women as we know them today. Camelot.

GENE: If technology can clone, technology can bring a cloned baby to term outside the body. The two worlds are equally possible.

GINA: Maybe, but not equally appealing.

GENE: Damn straight.

In Gina's All-Female World, There Would Be No:

Item	Reason
Grades of gasoline	Get "gas." Put in car. Go.
Stereo "systems," especially with meters that let you watch fluctuations of loudness	One price, $50. One switch: on-off.
Lawns	Gardens, yes. Turf, no.
Radio stations compulsively reporting the precise temperatures in six towns and at the airport, all of which are two miles and one degree Fahrenheit apart.	"It's cold. Dress warmly."
Noogies, wedgies, pantsing, towel flicking, goosing, finger pulling, Indian rope burning, pointing at the belly then finger-dragging up the nostril, armpit farting, knuckle cracking, bird flipping, palm-to-biceps fuck-you gesturing, whoopee cushions, rubber dog shit,	I mean, *please.*

rubber vomit, twitching rubber
rats in traps, public groin
scratching, groin yanking,
groin kneading, that car decal
of Calvin peeing, and loogies

Plus, in an all-woman world:

- A celebrated art form would be Keeping Photographs in Shoe Boxes.

- All beds would have "magic fingers."

- Computers would be equipped to hug you when you write something good.

- By law, grilled cheese sandwiches would be available 24/7 at all eating establishments, even five-star restaurants, of which there would be millions.

In Gene's All-Male World, There Would Be No:

Item	Reason
Potpourri, cologne, air fresheners, etc.	"Fragrance"—an unknown concept.
Bathtubs	Homes consist only of big, tiled rooms with hose couplings and drains in the middle. All chairs are plastic-covered recliners.

Napkins, facial tissues, sponges, toilet paper, bath towels, kitchen towels, potholders, oven mitts	All supplanted by paper towels sold in rolls the size of Doric columns
Padded clothes hangers	What, clothes feel pain?
Melba toast, tofu, puffed rice cakes	Federal law: Food must possess a taste.
Greeting cards	Just a note From me to say No guy writes This sissy way.
"Nice"	Word does not exist.
Melon ballers, butter pats with embossed designs, tea cozies, pillow shams, toilet brush caddies, bed skirts, tissue-box covers	These are "nice" things.
Vegetables	Most vitamin requirements met by pork products.
Cups, glasses	All beverages, including Mouton-Rothschild Lafite, consumed from container.

Plus, in an all-man world:

- Only female animals are neutered.
- In movie theaters, every other seat would be cordoned off, so no one could sit next to you.
- The only art form even faintly resembling ballet would be "the wave."
- Nobody would eat fruit unless he were sick.
- Masturbation would be a sacrament.

3

Are You Male or Female?
(Don't Be So Sure)

GENE: If you think you don't need this test, you're hopelessly out of date, stuck somewhere in the mid-twentieth century, when it was still considered a simple matter to tell whether a person was male or female: Back then, you just looked at his or her genitalia.

GINA: Her or his. There is no reason to give primacy to the male personal pronoun.

GENE: This system of sex typing through eyeballing naked people was employed most famously by doctors with the International Olympic Committee. The technology began to change in the late 1950s when medical science hurriedly started experimenting with DNA genetic typing so as to avoid having to look too hard at Tamara Press, that 220-pound Russian shot-putter who resembled an igloo with pubic hair.

Both techniques, of course, were your basic pass-fail tests. That seemed hunky-dory until the whole two-sex system was found to be inadequate, coinciding more or less with the discovery, in 1967, of Herbert "Tiny Tim" Khoury and his ukulele.

GINA: *Hunky-dory* is a ridiculous expression.

GENE: Stop interrupting.

GINA: It would be easier to stop interrupting if you got to your point more efficiently. The point you are ineptly attempting to make is that sex and gender are not the same thing.

GENE: I am?

GINA: Yes.

GENE: They're not?

GINA: No. Men never understand this. "Sex" is your equipment. "Gender" describes all the accompanying differences that typically attach to the two sexes, such as behavior, attitudes, social and cultural roles, and so forth. "Sex" is to "gender" as "brain" is to "mind." A homosexual transvestite may well be of the male sex and the female gender.

In recent years, psychologists have come to believe that one's gender basically exists on a sort of continuum, with Betty Boop on one end and Jesse Ventura on the other. The rest of us are in between.

These differences have always been around, but we failed to acknowledge them adequately or develop sophisticated vocabularies for them. Back in the 1950s, for example, we just understood that some women became phys ed teachers. It is when you begin to look at gender, and not just sex, that you get the Boop-Ventura Continuum. Betty is all the way on the left, Jesse all the way on the right.

GENE: Who comes right before Jesse Ventura?

GINA: That would be Jabba the Hutt.

GENE: And immediately after Betty Boop?

GINA: Michael Jackson. Then Olivia Newton-John.

GENE: So you contend it is no longer even sufficient to

say of someone that he or she is a man or a woman?

GINA: She or he. Right. You have to be sensitive to the existence of a more complex scale.

GENE: Actually, the media have been struggling with this issue for a while, with varying degrees of success. The need to display sensitivity sometimes collides with the requirement to provide information. A few years ago, *The Washington Post* ran a story about a lesbian couple that was adopting a child. It was a nice story, not at all judgmental, completely respectful of the rights of well-intentioned people to make alternative lifestyle choices and whatnot. The story was so sensitive and respectful that the writer found herself unable to ask a question that would have seemed indelicate. And so the story contained no reference whatsoever to the singular fact, quite evident from the accompanying photograph, that one of the mommies had a full, lush, unambiguous Saddam Hussein–style mustache.

GINA: Wow!

GENE: Rules are changing. Things are getting convoluted.

GINA: Do you know that some feminist linguists have actually proposed a number of new gender-neutral pronouns, single words to replace the cumbersome compound expressions "he or she," "him or her," and "himself or herself"? These include "zie" for "he or she," "zir" for "him or her," and "zirself" for "himself or herself." There are also various permutations of "per," as in "person," as in "perself."

GENE: You're kidding.

GINA: I am not.

GENE: That's idiotic.

GINA: Agreed. Language is not a plaything for the politically self-righteous.

GENE: I say they can all go fuck zirselves.

GINA: I would not have put it quite that way.

GENE: I know. And your score in the test below would reflect that particular aesthetic.

_____

Where Are You on the Boop-Ventura Continuum?

Circle all appropriate answers.

1. You might drive at 100 miles per hour if:
    a. Your child were bleeding to death and you had to get to the hospital.
    b. You were being pursued by a homicidal maniac.
    c. You had too much to drink.
    d. It was a rental.

2. You are a guest at a dinner party. After using the toilet facilities, you discover that there is no toilet tissue. You:
    a. Use your own facial tissues, and afterward discreetly mention the oversight to your hostess so that no one else will be inconvenienced.
    b. Use your own facial tissues, then rectify the problem on your own by resupplying the first bathroom with toilet tissue culled from elsewhere in the house.
    c. Leave as though nothing had happened and waddle off to another bathroom.
    d. Are cracking up because choice (b) said "rectify."

3. You are fat. This makes you feel:

   a. Suicidal.
   b. Awful.
   c. Fat.
   d. Feel?

4. A friend has set you up on a blind date with someone described, at the last minute, as having "a terrific sense of humor." Which of the following goes through your head first?

   a. "I hope I'll be able to get all the jokes!"
   b. "Perfect!"
   c. *"Whuh*-oh."
   d. A bullet.

5. To demonstrate your affection for your son, you call him

   a. "My little hero."
   b. "Sweetie."
   c. "Junior."
   d. Once every two months.

6. Dancing makes you feel:

   a. Like you are floating free through a moonlit sky.
   b. Like a woman.
   c. Stupid.
   d. Like a *%$& woman.

7. Gun control is:

    a. None of your business, really.

    b. Essential for the protection of society.

    c. An assault on individual rights.

    d. Essential for minimizing inaccuracy due to recoil.

8. When you see two men hugging, you assume:

    a. They are good friends.

    b. They are being reunited after a long separation.

    c. They are gay.

    d. They are Siamese twins.

9. You might bake a cake:

    a. Any old time.

    b. When there's a new recipe you want to try out.

    c. To impress a date, but only once.

    d. When trying to sneak a file into a federal penitentiary.

10. What is your favorite comfort food?

    a. Girl Scout Trefoil cookies.

    b. Frozen Sara Lee chocolate cake.

    c. Macaroni and cheese.

    d. Beer.

11. Bandera, Tex. (REUTERS)—A jury handed down a murder conviction today to a Texas man who shot and killed a longtime friend he accused of drinking the last beer in his refrigerator.

As a juror in this real court case, what key fact would you want to know before deciding on a sentence?

a. What sort of childhood abuse or neglect might have explained this man's unconscionable behavior?
b. Did the shooter have any history of violence?
c. Precisely how many beers were in the refrigerator two hours *prior* to the shooting?
d. So, did the guy *take* the beer or not?

12. You are given exactly five thousand dollars to spend on a single item for your home. You pick:

a. An eighteenth-century French armoire.
b. A six-burner Viking chef's stove.
c. A sectional sofa of fine Corinthian leather.
d. A TV the size of a UPS truck.

13. When filled, a cup holds a volume of 9 cubic inches. How much is that in cubic centimeters?

a. I don't know.
b. I don't care.
c. 148.
d. Less than a handful.

14. How would you remove a coffee stain from a nice silk shirt?

    a. Sodium bicarbonate and club soda.
    b. The dry cleaners.
    c. A soapy sponge.
    d. Windex.

15. What is the best tool to use to clear the snow off your car?

    a. Some guy.
    b. One of those ice-scraper/brush thingies.
    c. Your sleeve.
    d. Wind.

16. How do you pronounce *foyer, often,* and *endive*?

    a. Foy-YAY, OFF-ten, ON-deeve.
    b. Foy-YAY, OFF-un, EN-dive.
    c. FOY-er, OFF-un, EN-dive.
    d. Hall, a lot, lettuce.

17. *The Wizard of Oz* might have been an even better movie if:

    a. The flying monkeys were a little less scary.
    b. It could not have been a better movie.
    c. Toto was a Rottweiler.
    d. The ruby slippers "reflected up."

18. Hospital emergency rooms are reporting an alarming increase in serious injuries among persons under age twenty from accidents involving "potato bazookas." These are homemade contraptions constructed from a length of PVC pipe that has been sealed on one end, filled with a combustible liquid like hairspray or lighter fluid, and blocked on the other end by a potato or some other object that becomes a projectile expelled with enormous force when the liquid is ignited. Teenagers experimenting with potato bazookas have been seriously injured by potatoes, apples, toilet paper rolls, and even — most recently — a frog. What sort of persons do you think generally sustain these injuries?

    a. Totally deranged persons.
    b. Moronic, irresponsible jackasses.
    c. Boys.
    d. Boys denied sufficient training in the proper use of PVC-housed explosive devices.

19. What two words would best describe your favorite restaurant?

    a. Really cute.
    b. Wonderful food.
    c. Big portions.
    d. Place-mat menus.

20. Look down between your legs. What do you call this region of your body?

    a. My personal area.
    b. My crotch.
    c. My groin.
    d. My love muscle.

SCORING

Count one point for every (a) answer, two for every (b), three for every (c), and four for every (d).

Gina's scoring analysis:

I scored 46. In general, the lower your score, the higher your conventional femininity quotient. Understand, however, that gender is a complex and inexact measurement, and scoring particularly high or particularly low does not necessarily correlate with masculinity or femininity as we have come to understand them. Above all, feel good about yourself and your choices.

Gene's scoring analysis:

I scored 76. Under 65 means you are either a woman or a wuss.

4

Men and Women Are Funny. Just Not to Each Other.

GINA: As is already obvious—and will become increasingly more so as Gene tries and fails to get broad acceptance of jokes about death, genitalia, and excreta—men and women find different things funny.

GENE: You said *broad* acceptance.

GINA: That's not funny.

GENE: Yes, it is.

GINA: The question is, are these gender differences innate or learned?

GENE: Learned.

GINA: Because . . . ?

GENE: Because when you cover your face with your hands and then remove your hands and say "peekaboo!" with a stupidly astonished expression, infants of both sexes will laugh. And at that age they will laugh at nothing else.

GINA: So?

GENE: So that means there is a point at which our senses of

humor are tabulae rasae except for this most basic, hardwired humor reflex. Peekaboo is a phenomenon that spans oceans, ethnicities, systems of political belief. Presbyterian and Jewish babies laugh at peekaboo. Hutu *and* Tutsi babies laugh at peekaboo. Communist babies laugh at peekaboo. Peekaboo tickles before tickling tickles—but most to the point, it tickles not only before any gender-role brainwashing has occurred but before the baby even knows it *has* a gender.

GINA: And this is significant because . . . ?

GENE: It is significant because peekaboo represents the principle behind all humor: the sudden introduction of a conflicting frame of reference. It expresses the concept "Whoa—that wasn't there before!"

All humor, whether sophomoric or sophisticated, contains this basic element at its core. ("Take my wife—please" is funny because you suddenly realize the reference point is not the one you assumed it to be.) And here we have peekaboo—this essential principle distilled to its most primitive form—slaying girl and boy babies in equal number. It is the first and last moment of such humor parity; ergo we can conclude that sometime shortly afterward some environmental factor intercedes to give females their famously cruddier sense of humor.

GINA: That's not funny.

GENE: Yes, it is. We put skirts on girls, and everything changes. Suddenly is birthed the Giggle.

GINA: I do not defend the Giggle. The Giggle has enslaved girls for centuries. But it is an understandable adaptation in a society that permits boys but not girls to take risks. Boys are rewarded for rambunctious behavior, but girls are encouraged to be demure and restrained. There are actually studies on this. So boys become aggressive with everything, including humor. Their laughter is liberated from social sanctions. They guffaw.

Girls, however, become situationally dependent—before they laugh, they look to see if anyone else is laughing. Since they seek permission to laugh, laughter becomes an act of sedition; thus, the dreadful semiapologetic giggle. Then this weakness morphs into the adolescent girlish convention? Of inflecting statements? As though they were questions? Seeking approval? Sounding like imbeciles? Even if they are asking? About whether they should go to Harvard? Or Yale? Medical School?

GENE: You seem to be making my point for me.

GINA: I am not. Girls eventually mature. Boys do not.

GENE: I stipulate that boys mature more slowly.

GINA: I am shocked.

GENE: Men do not ignore the plainly evident just because it happens to be annoying or inconvenient. Maturation occurs at an unequal rate. On my daughter Molly's first birthday, we invited my friend Mike over for a little party. Mike's son, Matthew, had also just turned one year old. Molly sat on my lap and as I turned the pages of a picture book, I asked her to point to recognizable images. "Where's the baby?" I said, and Molly pointed to the picture of the baby. "Where's the daddy?" I said, and Molly pointed to the picture of the daddy. "Where's the shrill, castrating female?" I said, and my wife whacked me with a spatula. The point is, from start to finish it was a pretty impressive display for a one-year-old.

After I was done I looked up at Mike and smiled. It was a challenge, not unlike those vaudeville tap-dance challenges where one tapster executes a routine, then theatrically gestures to the other, who slickly outdoes him. So Mike put Matthew on his knee and opened a book. Matthew began to eat the book.

GINA: Exactly. Men are still eating the book. In my experience, human males go from immaturity straight to dotage.

GENE: *Maturity* is a code word for humorlessness.

GINA: Only to the immature. Here is what happens: Our society gives women the responsibility for maintaining an orderly, domestic world within a sphere of chaos and uncertainty. If you are going to raise non-psychotic children into adulthood, you have to make it your business *not* to keep switching frames of reference on them.

GENE: I used to tell my kids that the horsie goes moo.

GINA: Of course you did. When he was traveling to another city with his then-teenage sons and the boys went off to explore, my husband used to deliberately give them the wrong address for their hotel, on the theory that "adventure is good." Women do not do this. Women have to create the illusion of a stable, non-threatening world. It is an illusion, and we know it, but it is our job to maintain it.

GENE: So you lose your sense of humor.

GINA: You do not. A woman's sense of humor becomes more complex and layered. It is based on an appreciation of the absurdity of the human condition, whereas a man's sense of humor is based upon the concept that farts are funny.

GENE: Farts *are* funny. And farts are funny precisely because of the absurdity of the human condition. Even Chaucer understood this.

GINA: Chaucer, to my literary recollection, was a man.

GENE: Immaterial. There is and always has been a sophisticated philosophical underpinning to the humor of bodily functions.

Humor in general exists mostly as a defense mechanism. We use it to reduce our existential anxieties by laughing at the things that disturb us: not only the arbitrary nature of death, which has birthed an entire body of tasteless space-shuttle-explosion-type humor, but also the knowledge that we are deeply flawed as a species.

We are hypocritical, we are egotistical, we are manipulative, we are pompous, we are selfish, we do stupid things. So poking fun at these traits make us laugh. Above all, our species clings desperately to a perception of ourselves as dignified and civilized—we distance ourselves from the horned beasts and the coelacanths and whatnot. And yet we still have to do these ridiculous, animal acts. Farting explodes an essential pretension of our lives. We laugh at that realization. It's why sex is funny, too.

GINA: Sex *is* funny. But not because of why men think it's funny.

GENE: Sex is funny because it features two highly evolved life forms—think Marie Curie and Pliny the Elder—engaging in an act slightly less dignified than a grand mal seizure, utilizing facial expressions that would shame a capuchin monkey.

GINA: Sex is not slapstick.

GENE: Sex is most assuredly slapstick.

GINA: Sex is funny because it is an exercise in appetite, and all appetite is funny. What's funny about sex is what we do to obtain it.

Go to a restaurant. Observe and eavesdrop. Let's say you see a nicely dressed couple, heads together, engaged in animated conversation that veers effortlessly from the global imperatives of alternative energy sources to an assessment of the emerging trends in rock music to the hermeneutic examination of the eschatological nature of the teachings of the historical Jesus. You can pretty much conclude that this couple has not yet Done It. The married couple is over there in the corner, trying to remember if they need to buy fabric softener for the dryer. Their dialogue is static cling, which, now that I think of it, kind of defines long-term relationships. It's unavoidable.

My husband and I teach college English, and people sometimes say to us, "Oh, you two smart and learned people, you must have the most amazing conversations!" Do you know what conversations we have? He will have his head in the refrigerator and he will ask, "Do we have any cream cheese?" Why does he think I have memorized the contents of the refrigerator? Let me ask you, who do you think would be the best authority on the contents of the refrigerator at any given moment—the person in the living room or the person who, at that very moment, is inspecting the contents of the refrigerator?

GENE: I'm trying to parse that last response of yours. I am trying to figure out how you veered from point A to point B.

GINA: See, a woman would have no trouble with this. It is not veering, it is dancing. Men hate to dance. This is the difference between the male and female senses of humor. When a woman tells you she has something funny to tell you, if you're smart you pull up a chair and reach for a Diet Coke. You're there for the duration. The story sashays from point to point. There are sometimes footnotes. The humor is situational, juxtapositional, implicit, absurdist, internally referential. Whereas when you go up to a man and say you have something funny to tell him, he holds up a stopwatch and says, "Go!" He thinks it has to be something he can repeat to other men in the hallway. He is looking for a punch line, a quickie, a bada-*bing*. Women want an extended experience, a kneading, rolling, stroking process. Our humor doesn't come to one particular point of release.

GENE: You're getting me hot here.

GINA: Take a cold bath.

GENE: I can't. It would be irresponsible. We're in a drought. Which reminds me, some female readers complained the other day when I held a humor contest in *The Washington Post* to come up with really, really inappropriate tips for conserving water during the drought. They were upset with an example I published.

GINA: Which was?

GENE: "When drowning puppies, use the toilet, not the bathtub."

GINA: That's not funny.

GENE: Yes, it is.

You know there's a humor gap in your relationship when:

❥ Your favorite amusing book is *Les Liaisons Dangereuses* and his is *Snappy Answers to Stupid Questions*.

❥ Your favorite serious book is *Wuthering Heights* and his is *Snappy Answers to Stupid Questions*.

❥ Your wife is so proud of you that among gatherings of friends and colleagues, she likes to retell jokes you have told her. She does this by flapping her wrists in that cute way that would seem really effeminate in a man, and then announcing the punch line, as in "You know how horses have these long faces? Well" [flap], this horse walks into a bar, and . . ."

❥ Your husband thinks "Henry Wadsworth Longfellow" is the funniest name on the face of the earth, and does not understand why this makes him an idiot.

5

Pulp Friction

GENE: Men and women write differently. I would never pre-sume to suggest that men write "better" because that would belie the obvious fact that some of the most important writers in history were women. I am thinking in particular of Lucille Dick-ens, Darlene Shakespeare, and Margaret "Mufsy" Martinez-Yeats. Not to mention Mark Twain, which, as every schoolchild knows, was a pen name for the famous satirist Agnes Plotnick.

GINA: Please tell me you are not seriously arguing that women haven't contributed hugely to English-language literature.

GENE: On the contrary. I acknowledge that they have. The Brontë sisters alone have filled bookshelves with enormous mounds of feathery, pompadoured literature no male has ever read. Once, I am told, a well-intentioned man actually forced himself to plow through several consecutive pages of *Jane Eyre* and, tragically, began to menstruate.

GINA: Your ignorance is breathtaking.

GENE: Do you deny that, by and large, male writers are read by men and women, while female writers are read by women?

GINA: I do not deny it.

GENE: Do you think we might conclude that women's writing is of parochial appeal?

GINA: I think we might not. Men will not read books by women because, unlike women, men tend toward intellectual cowardice, feeling secure only with themes familiar to them. They will not find such familiar things in books by women, in which people go through life without getting shot, becoming impotent, chasing large sea mammals, traveling through time and/or space in powerful vehicles, or killing Hitler.

Women writers, as you point out, are concerned with feathery, pompadoured things: birth, death, marriage, friendship. Girly stuff. Moreover, women do not mind an occasional sentence with a dependent clause or two and no exclamation points. You don't have. To write. Everything. Like this!

GENE: I can see how you would prefer the artistry of Danielle Steel to the work of a hack like Hemingway.

GINA: Hemingway is the premature ejaculator of American literature.

GENE: That's cold.

GINA: Thank you. The fact is, the differences between male and female writing are enormous. They involve language, character depth, subject matter, even titles. No woman would ever write a book called *Around the World in Eighty Days*. No woman wants to go around the world in eighty days. Do you know how much packing and unpacking you would have to do? You want to stop, go shopping, sample the food.

Many years ago at Dartmouth, a female professor was teaching Erica Jong's *Fear of Flying*. The class had been reading all the usual contemporary writers like Mailer, Updike, and Cheever, so this was entirely new ground. The professor assigned a male student and a female student to stand up and summarize the book. The young woman said that she'd found it delightful and refreshing in the way it spoke to women's experiences. She loved Isadora Wing for both her strengths and her insecurities, and laughed at how she unexpectedly gets her period in the middle of Paris and must duck-walk around until she finds a tampon.

Then the male student got up and expressed his outrage at the previous interpretation. Reading, he said, is not a gendered experience. He said that he, too, felt just as sympathetic with, and connected to, Isadora Wing as he would be to an E. L. Doctorow character. He said that Isadora's concerns were about being a human, not being a woman, and that they spoke to him directly. And as to the other issue, he said contemptuously, "Do you think men don't know what happens to a woman's body every other month?"

GENE: Excellent. I acknowledge men can be idiots, particularly callow young men attempting sophistication. But what's your point?

GINA: My point is that men and women are so different in their experiences that there is a mutual exclusivity in their writing. It is incompatible.

GENE: Okay. Maybe that's why so few books are written by a man *and* a woman.

GINA: This one is.

GENE: Right. But look at the hash we're making of it.

GINA: True.

GENE: Plus, we get to fight. Imagine if a man and a woman tried to write a novel as a team, together.

GINA: Hmm.

GENE: I'll start.

GINA: What are the ground rules?

GENE: We take alternating paragraphs and have to build on what came before.

A Novel
By Gene and Gina

GENE: Chisholm groaned himself awake, his head rolling slow and ugly, like a cement mixer with thudding slop inside. His mouth told him he'd spent the night either licking rickshaw tires in a Singapore slum or plying too many cheap women with too much expensive bourbon. Either way, all he'd managed to pick up was a lot of no leads on the case of his life. He grabbed his gat from a dresser drawer, filled it with bye-bye pills, set his fedora at an angle he hoped was cocky, and went out into the sneer of a morning sun that didn't give a crap about has-been private dicks blowing their one last chance at a big payday.

GINA: The scent of lilacs wafted down the tree-lined street as Jake lifted his tired, importuning eyes to the sky. Yes, the sun was harsh, but the breeze was cool and carried the faint hint of renewal in the early June day. For the first time in months, Jake allowed himself to remember Rebecca, the girl he'd loved twenty years before, when he was in the first blush of youth, when his soul was as clean and new as this morning. After all these years, he still hungered for her, for her carillon laughter, for the embrace that welcomed his sharp edges and softened them with its self-lessness. Where was she now? Shouldn't that be the most important "case" on his agenda?

GENE: Nah.

GINA: Jake didn't see the car until it was too late, and he couldn't get the license plate without those glasses he'd had to start wearing since he turned forty-five, the glasses he unwisely kept tucked away inside the pocket of his unbecoming silk-and-worsted sports jacket, which he'd bought when the young salesgirl told him its dark color brought out the fire in his amber eyes. Perhaps he should start shopping with women his own age instead of taking advice from some barely postadolescent floozy who steals glances and husbands with equal casualness. Anyhoo, as the car sped around the corner, the back door opened and a man's body rolled onto the pavement.

GENE: No, it wasn't a man. It was dressed to look like a man, but a goat can't impersonate a fish. There was no hiding the generous curves beneath the cheap suit, the sort of curves that belong to the sort of woman who turns a man into a sap with the careless flash of a calf. And she wasn't real young, okay? It's not like Chisholm was some freaking child molester, for crying out loud; he just liked women who like to do the sorts of things to men that men like having done to them by women who like being women. The point being that she was a real looker, except for the ax that had split her like Excalibur. The body was deader than Dostoyevsky, and just as hard to read.

GINA: Not, of course, that Jake had much practice reading women, at least not in the last twenty years. Bimbos and hookers are a short, quick read, like a washing instruction tag, and about as satisfying. "Poor kid," he thought, sadly surveying the devastation at his feet. Then he looked again. It was Rebecca! Regret and remorse washed over him, drowning him in incomprehensible sorrow. Actually, it would have been comprehensible had he been the rare sort of man with some inclination toward introspection, some internal topography, a life within that recognized its emotional core. Still, something took hold. Jake heard a sound like a mournful wail, like a thousand grieving voices raised in agony, and he realized it was coming from him. Maybe it wasn't too late for him. Maybe this tragedy might awaken that part of him that yearned for release. He swore by all that was holy that this was a murder he was going to solve.

GENE: After all, when a private dick gets some dame's body flung at his feet, it's a challenge to his manhood.

GINA: Manhood that, as he may or may not have known, is completely defined by one's willingness to openly express one's vulnerability.

GENE: Accidentally stepping on the stiff's face but not giving a damn, Chisholm commandeered a passing cab. "Follow that car," he barked, pointing at the taillights growing smaller in the distance.

GINA: Deep down, Jake realized that he was so upset and filled with sadness that he was thinking irrationally and his priorities were all askew.

GENE: This made him think of Reuben Askew, the former governor of Florida. God, Chisholm hated pols—filthy, grasping swine, all of them. Just like the crooked congressman he was being paid serious simoleons to nail—that is, before some stupid skirt turned up dead and ruined everything. Sure, his priorities were askew. What was he doing in this cab, chasing nothing more certain than a bellyful of lead?

GINA: Suddenly Jake looked up to see that the cabdriver was Luisa, his lap dancer from the night before! "I can see that you're trying desperately to turn your life around!" Jake yelled through the Plexiglas divider. He was stunned, humbled, and inspired by her indomitable will. She was a terrific driver, too.

GENE: That night they had sex, so the case turned out swell.

6

Cooking, Washing, and Irony

GENE: Here is an interesting paradox about women. Although most will readily admit that they are no good at the physical sciences, and largely ignorant of Euclidean geometry, every last one has somehow mastered the seemingly impossible maneuver of removing a bra from under a sweater. There's some fumbling, elbows fly, and *squadoosh*—the bra floops out the front or comes snaking out the armhole. No man on earth knows how it is done. Can you share the secret?

GINA: No.

GENE: No?

GINA: No.

GENE: Okay, here's another interesting irony. Do you know the name of Evelyn Waugh's first wife?

GINA: I don't care.

GENE: It was Evelyn! Evelyn Waugh, the writer, was married to Evelyn Waugh, the homemaker and distant descendant of Henry VII. Within that single marriage, we have a fascinating gender phenomenon in microcosm. Why is it that through history, women have appropriated classic men's names with impunity? Shirley! Beverly! Joyce! Ashley! Toby! Vivian! Jody! Meredith! It goes on through the generations, willy-nilly. Women have already stolen Willy, and Nilly would be next if it were a man's name. The larceny continues unabated to this day. I know of a little girl named Spencer. But the opposite is not true. You don't suddenly see little boys being named Dorcas or Tiffany. Why is that?

GINA:

GENE: You have to participate here. This chapter is about gender ironies.

GINA: No, it isn't. This chapter is Part II of the last chapter, about fiction. This is Part II of "Pulp Friction."

GENE: There is no Part II of "Pulp Friction."

GINA: Chapter Six: Pulp Friction, Part II.

There is now.

Gene: We exhausted this subject.

GINA: We did not. You took advantage of me.

GENE: How?

GINA: You started the story, which means I had to live with your stupid tough-guy plot. I was forced into a no-win, defensive posture. This time, I want control of the narrative.

GENE: It won't change the outcome.

GINA: We'll see.

A Second Novel
By Gina and Gene

GINA: What had started as a casual evening between two new acquaintances was turning into so much more. Over the hours in the cozy pub, Nickie and Jared shared their pasts—Nickie, her schoolgirl crushes; Jared, the sweetness of his beloved childhood pets. And finally Jared told her, in a subdued tone, about the recent death of his father, the man who had reared him as best he could with what little he had, hauling the boy around the country on sales trips, like a small samples case with a cowlick. His mother, it seems, had decided she would be happier with a more exciting man in a more exciting place, and so departed one morning, leaving a note scrawled on a paper bag that held the remains of yesterday's takeout Chinese. Nickie was beginning to understand something, and it intrigued her: To such a man, "home" must be a magical concept.

GENE: She might actually be attracted to Jared, Nickie thought, if only she liked men. Her tastes ran to statuesque brunettes with full bodices and small tattoos in beguiling places—like the pouty temptress at the table against the wall, pretending to be amused by her wealthy, balding date but throwing Nickie a look that scalded in a not unpleasant way. Nickie realized that the tail end of her evening might wind up being just that—a night spent in a most explicit rendezvous with a most unexpected partner, and with Jared, perhaps, as a most interested observer.

GINA: Nickie swiftly dismissed these thoughts. She was

too strong and serious a woman to be enslaved by body chemistry, nor would she even *think* about matters of the flesh during the next several hours, which happened to coincide precisely with the length of this novel. This was to be all business. Nickie realized that this man sitting across the table had what she needed, what every headstrong woman needs at some point in her life: a law degree and a convincing swagger. As the country's most prominent and sought-after surgical oncologist, Nickie needed Jared, or someone very much like him, to represent her in a lawsuit against a rapacious pharmaceutical conglomerate. Literally billions of dollars were at stake. If she succeeded, thousands of sick and dying underprivileged children would have a new chance at life, and some giant medical reputations would deflate like a soufflé in an earthquake.

GENE: Caught as he was in some tedious, chick-driven narrative sodden with interminable interior monologues, Jared did not appreciatively assess Nickie's contours, as he might have in some other, more imaginative literary form. Nor did he stop to ponder the stupidity of his name, which sounded phony baloney, like he was Superman's uncle back on Krypton or something. Not to mention "Nickie," a name that was yet another flagrant example of gyno-banditry. Instead, dutifully obeying rules he did not fully understand, he carefully weighed the desperation in Nickie's eyes and waited patiently for her, finally, to speak, to utter a sound, a few sentences contained within quotation marks, a morsel of dialogue for the benefit of readers starving for scene, presence, action, and some hint of personality.

GINA: And as it happens, Nickie proceeded to do precisely that, laying out her proposal with the sort of direct eloquence that characterized the way she, and many successful women, conduct themselves in matters of business.

GENE: Jared was impressed.

GINA: "He is?" thought Nickie suspiciously.

GENE: Yes, indeed he was, Jared realized. If there were the opposite of a hired killer, it was this person seated across from him—this powerful, capable, yet somehow vulnerable woman who earned more in a week than he did in a year by finding death in a person and slicing it out. Nick the Knife. He felt excited, almost honored, that she needed him. Overcome with emotion and genuine admiration, he smiled. Across from him, Nickie stiffened, mistaking his innocent reaction for a tawdry come-on. "This pig is no different from all other men," Nickie thought unfairly, not realizing—as many women do not—the ugliness of such knee-jerk gender stereotyping. Imperiously, Nickie stood to leave.

GINA: And she would have left, too, for she had seen this sort of self-righteous self-deception before in men—in which they truly believed they were showing sensitivity but in fact were engaged in the age-old male practice of turning any situation, even a straightforward business proposition, into a referendum about *them*. So yes, Nickie was about to leave when she caught a look in Jared's eye, a faint flicker of remorse, so uncommon in a man and therefore so refreshing. Clearly he knew he was in the wrong. Nickie sat.

GENE: Jared sat, too. He just sat there. Because that's what they were doing, sitting and feeling things. Methodically surveying and cataloguing all of his emotions, past and present, Jared suddenly felt something new. At first he could not place it, but then it hit him in the face. No, *hit* was too active a verb. It softly brushed his face, like a crinoline curtain bestirred by a brisk summer wind. It was the inescapable fact that nothing whatsoever had occurred in the last half hour. Nothing! Jared stood up suddenly, upsetting the table and the literary form. "Dammit," he bellowed, his words breaking the stillness with the defiant authority of a power fart in a confessional. "What is *wrong* with you people? Can't you see that a story needs *action?* What do you want from me, woman? You want to sue somebody? Let's do it! I'll squeeze someone till he explodes like a ketchup packet under a hobnail boot! I'll hound a man in court until he commits suicide with a rusty fisherman's gaff. Anything! Action! Let's *do* something! Get into a car chase! Rob a convenience store and pistol-whip the clerk! Stomp a wino! Hijack a bus! Shoot someone!"

GINA: Nickie regarded this curious man with frank interest as she calmly and wordlessly reapplied her lipstick. Yes, she thought, the distraught fellow had a point. It happens occasionally—rarely, perhaps by accident, but it happens nonetheless—that the human male will entirely on his own come up with an idea that is at once logical, persuasive, and wise. Jared was right. Sometimes action does speak more effectively than words. So she shot him.

GENE: Feel better now?

GINA: Yes, I do.

GENE: There's nothing like a little humor back-and-forth, eh?

GINA: Having humor together can be a nice thing.

GENE: It can relieve tension.

GINA: Yes.

GENE: So you're not mad anymore?

GINA: No. That worked out well. I'm satisfied.

GENE: Make-up humor. It's the best kind.

7

You and I Make Whee

GENE: Did you see that weird clause in our book contract?

GINA: I haven't seen the contract.

GENE: Then you should be getting it tomorrow. Al just mailed us the final copy.

GINA: Al?

GENE: Our agent. The contract has this great provision.

GINA: Why haven't I met him? If I don't get to meet you, I should at least meet our agent.

GENE: I haven't met him either. No one ever meets Al. Al's been my agent for six years. He's very good, but I have no idea what he looks like. He lives somewhere in Pennsylvania, or possibly New Jersey. I've only talked to him four or five times, because he doesn't like to use the phone. He sends me letters by U.S. Mail.

GINA: C'mon.

GENE: Honest. Al doesn't own a computer. He uses a typewriter, with correction tape.

GINA: This is a very typically male thing.

GENE: What are you talking about? Men love technology.

GINA: Yes, but they love technology mostly because it permits them to avoid intimacy. The history of modern technology is an organized retreat from intimate communication. Radio extinguished the hearth, replacing the need for conversation. TV delivered concrete imagery, removing the element of imagination and thus even further truncating debate, discussion, analysis. And now, e-mail.

Men love e-mail because it means they don't have to use the phone, which might create a situation in which they have to spontaneously express an emotion or react honestly to an observation. E-mail is quick, but it is not spontaneous—it maintains distance and permits dissimulation.

GENE: Can I tell you about our contract?

GINA: My point is that our agent has taken this avoidance reaction, this impulse toward aloofness, and carried it to the extreme. He is too aloof even for e-mail. This is basic developmental psychology. It's innately male.

The first thing a newborn baby knows is "I'm biting some toes." Next, it's "I'm biting *my* toes." That is the first sense of self. And you know what happens next? The baby looks at his or her mother and realizes, "This person is not part of me. This person is something else. It goes away sometimes." But next comes the important developmental pivot that creates Al, our agent, as the prototype of all men.

Little drooly baby Al doesn't have a tooth in his head yet. He has barely drawn his first breath, but he is already drawing conclusions. He looks at his mother and thinks, "I am not like this thing that hugs me and feeds me and makes little cooing noises as she wipes my scrawny butt and powders it with stuff that makes me smell like a medicinal lollipop. No, I am like that *other* thing, the one that comes home at five o'clock, turns on the TV, and drinks a whiskey sour."

From an early age, boys realize that to establish an identity, they must distance themselves from the primary person in their life. Thus, little baby Al creates a boundary. This is not true of his sister, Alice, who recognizes in her mother something like herself, and whose initial impulse is thereby inclusion and connection. It is why women go to the bathroom in pairs. What about the contract?

GENE: Huh?

GINA: Our contract. Did you lose your train of thought?

GENE: It got derailed. Feminist terrorists planted dynamite on the tracks. Page four of our contract discusses ancillary rights, specifically how we retain the ability to sell this book for other potential purposes. These purposes, as enumerated in the contract, include "dramatic, motion picture, radio, TV and theme parks."

GINA: Theme parks?

GENE: That's what it says! I'd like to find out what that means, too, so I'm going to fire off an emergency communiqué to Al. We should have our answer in eight, nine days, max.

GINA: Well, it's pretty clear to me what it means. It means that once this book becomes a runaway bestseller and our faces are as familiar to Americans as Mickey and Minnie, some venture capitalist will get the bright idea to wipe out some wetlands somewhere and build a theme park. Gene&GinaLand. It's practically a done deal. We should start planning the attractions.

GENE: Obviously, we'd have to start with the basics: a log flume plunge into the tunnel of love.

GINA: Oh, that ride would cost a *lot*.

GENE: Tell me about it.

GINA: You'd first have to go through the Hall of Old Girl-friends. . . .

GENE: I didn't mean *literally* tell me about it.

GINA: The image of each old girlfriend would be projected onto a fun-house mirror, so they'd have these absolutely enormous behinds, and you'd have to explain to your date, in detail, one by one, why she is better than each of them. As André Gide said, "It is not enough to be loved—I wish to be preferred."

GENE: We've already established that you are better-educated than I am. There's no need to start quoting French philosophers.

GINA: He was not a philosopher. He was a novelist and playwright, b. 1869, d. 1951.

GENE:

GINA: Well, I'm not the one getting facts wrong.

GENE: You know, I'm thinking Gene&GinaLand needs a Guess Your Weight booth. It would be mandatory. With a scale, for verification.

GINA: How about a ride only for women, called Big Is Better-land? It would be a fantasy ride, if you see what I mean.

GENE: That's nasty.

GINA: You started it.

GENE: Did not.

GINA: See, we're on the carousel right now. You keep going around in circles, only instead of music, it has the same droning argument, over and over.

GENE: The Marry-Go-Round! "We always do everything you want to do." "We do not." "Yes, we do." "Let's just forget it and make love." "We always do everything you want to do. . . ."

GINA: I'd like a Hall of Guys Who Will Dance with You. Or bumper cars. With bumper cars, you're *supposed* to dent a fender. No one yells at you.

GENE: Stick shift only.

GINA: Very funny.

GENE: Okay, how about the Emotional Roller Coaster?

GINA: The Emotional Roller Coaster would be operated by men, and only women would be allowed on. It would make you want to throw up. Women never put men on Emotional Roller Coasters. Women put men through Haunted Houses. Women spring sudden, really scary notions that always catch men flat-footed. "I was minding my own business when . . ." Did you ever notice that men are always saying that? "I was minding my own business when, *wham,* right out of the blue she asks me if I agree that any man my age is a sicko if he finds Britney Spears sexy." Women run the Haunted House.

GENE: I guess the carnies would pretty much stay the same. Pimply narcotics addicts with cigarette packs tucked up in the sleeves of their T-shirts.

GINA: No.

GENE: It's a good system. It's worked for millennia. Roman circuses were probably run by pimply narcotics addicts with cigarette packs tucked up in the sleeves of their togas.

GINA: Gene&GinaLand needs to appeal equally to women, and women have a problem with that sort of thing. It's a bad role model.

GENE: No one looks to carnies as role models for their kids.

GINA: That's not what I mean. Every year near where I live, the city of Willimantic, Connecticut, hosts a cheesy little traveling carnival. You know the type. Ferris wheel held together by old jockstraps, sno-cones that are too watery but you're afraid to complain to the tattoos, people with very poor eyesight doing the safety controls, and cleft-palate children running around.

So I'm there with my husband, Michael, and I'm telling him how sorry I feel for these poor people, that their lives must be awful—sweeping into a new town every week in a rootless, meaningless itinerant existence, with no families, no permanence—a demimonde of Flannery O'Connor characters subsisting on a diet of cherry slushes and fried dough with powdered sugar, getting drunk on cheap beer and bourbon night after night and having empty, unsafe sexual encounters with people they don't even know. And as I'm talking, I'm noticing that Michael is getting this wistful look in his eyes. He's practically tearing up, like a man who is realizing that he has missed his calling in life. He has become a man to whom teaching a class two mornings a week suddenly seems like a job on the assembly line in a chicken abattoir.

So, no carnies. Bad role model for husbands. You want women to show up, Gene&GinaLand has to be staffed by cheerful, clean young people working their way through Stanford. Plus, wholesome rides.

GENE: Well, I'd insist on a couple of Himalayas.

GINA: What are they?

GENE: Those sleek silver trains that roar around in a circle past really bad paintings of mountains and kids in lederhosen while they bellow Top-40 tunes and blast AC in your face.

GINA: What does that have to do with anything?

GENE: It doesn't. I just happen to like them. Also, those rotating drums that flatten you out against the sides, then the floor drops away. They've been known to get stuck in the on position at full speed, and people get sick and puke, and the puke slowly shivers its way around the drum, and you're trapped.

GINA: That's disgusting.

GENE: I know. I love those things.

GINA: Well, I have to admit they're appropriate for Gene&GinaLand. They put your relationship into total paralysis through the sheer weight of inertia. You're up against the wall, no support system, flattened into inaction by children, your mortgage, your terror of being alone, your disinclination to break in someone new who will tolerate your washing out pantyhose in the sink. We could call it the Inertia-tron.

GENE: Actually, it would be called the Centrifuge. What you're discussing is centrifugal force, which is a theoretical construct to explain the inverse of centripetal force, which is the tendency of an object to be pulled toward the center of a rotation. Centrifugal force is calculated the same way, through the formula $F_c = mv^2/r$, where m is mass, v is velocity, and r is the radius of the circle. It may well create a *state* of inertia, but let's not oversimplify the process or misstate the principles. Lady, this is Physics 101.

GINA:

GENE: Well, I'm not the one getting the facts wrong.

GINA: When women exit Big is Betterland, maybe they need a dose of a reality-based ride called It's a Small World After All.

GENE: Is that all you have in your arsenal?

GINA: Is that all you have in yours?

GENE: That's nasty.

GINA: You started it.

GENE: Did not.

Other Offerings from Gene&Gina Enterprises, Inc.

Gene&Gina Petting Zoo

Features baby goats, llamas, and sheep. Women are issued cups with pellets of food, and baby bottles of warm milk. Men are issued Daisy pellet rifles, and complimentary beer.

Gene&Gina Mall

Women's side has an assortment of boutiques offering free samples of one-of-a-kind products. Men's side is one big store where all products are arranged in strict alphabetical order. Beer is free.

Gene&Gina Hospital

Women's wing offers many plants, soothing lighting, comfortable furniture, and professional wellness consultants who offer advice about how to feel good about taking care of yourself. The doctors specialize in herbal remedies. There are no injections.

Men's wing looks like Jiffy Lube, only less complicated. Guys in overalls and rubber gloves hang around drinking coffee until they are needed to perform a procedure. These are the doctors. Nurses look like 1950s-era stewardesses. There are a lot of candy stripers in little caps. Beer is free.

Gene&Gina Fitness Club

On the women's side, you can choose whatever upbeat music you need to get you moving: salsa, oldies, disco, contemporary urban. The atmosphere is less like a gym than a great party where everybody is thoroughly, enthusiastically, and unselfconsciously swept up into a celebration of movement and music.

On the men's side there are weight machines, rowing machines, stair machines, batters' boxes with pitching machines, basketball-game arcade machines that go "da-*daah*" when you score, dartboards, pool tables, and free beer. No talking is permitted.

Gene&Gina Airlines
Women fly free, but they must wear short, tight-fitting dresses, cheap perfume, fishnet stockings, and shoes that come to a sharp point in the middle of the toes. Oddly, both men and women warily accept this arrangement. Beer is free.

Gene&Gina Shoe Emporia
Gina's occupies a twenty-acre territory no more than fifteen minutes from the heart of every major city. Stock changes daily. Salespeople encourage you to buy comfortable, beautiful shoes, many of which can be modified immediately to your specifications. They serve canapés and wine spritzers.

Gene's is a separate establishment, located behind an OTB parlor. It has two aisles: black and brown. You can also buy sneakers, but you have to know somebody. Free beer.

Gene&Gina Supreme Court
Gina's has sixty-one members with representation from a variety of demographics: There are female judges, male judges, lesbian judges, gay judges, black judges, Hispanic judges, Asian judges, Jewish judges, judges over 70, under 40, from rural areas, urban

areas, suburban areas, from poor families, rich families, fat, skinny, with good hair, bad hair, funny voices, big feet, small feet, AA members, former ballerinas, etc.

Gene's has two guys, one wearing black shoes, one wearing brown. If there's a tie, they bring in the guy with the sneakers. Naturally, there is free beer.

Gene&Gina Correctional Facility

Gina's system would rely on education and self-discipline to help the miscreant learn new ways to cope with the inequities and pressures of life outside. Learning self-respect and useful skills would permit those outside the law to be admitted as fully functioning citizens once their debt to society was paid. Oh, and rapists would be castrated.

Gene's prison would feature weight machines, rowing machines, stair machines, batters' boxes with pitching machines, basketball-game arcade machines that go "da-*daah*" when you score, dartboards, pool tables. No beer.

8

Why We Are Screwed:
The Inordinate Importance
of Sex

GENE: As we've seen, the reason that men and women have such intractable problems relating to each other is sex.

GINA: Wrong.

GENE: Wrong?

GINA: It is not the act itself. It is what comes before and after. It is the desire for it. The anticipation of it. The preparation for it. The strategizing over it. The discordance over the significance of it. The disjuncture over continuing appetites for it. The systematic use, misuse, and abuse of power to obtain or avoid it. Not to mention the consequences of it, which can reverberate until one is toothless.

GENE: In brief, then, we are talking about sex.

GINA: Well, yes.

GENE: Sheesh.

GINA: Sex creates a disproportionate atmosphere of tension

over what should be a straightforward transaction. It creates a mutual pathology of behavior. It makes men crazy, jealous, frustrated, uncontrollably voyeuristic, and competitive to an absurd degree. It makes women manipulative, coquettish, uncontrollably exhibitionist, and bizarrely self-destructive.

It explains why a woman who would never, for example, consider learning to ride a unicycle will nonetheless spend years perfecting the art of balancing on patent leather spikes that maim her feet. It explains the hysterical comb-over, the more hysterical toupee, and the most hysterical billion-dollar hair-loss-denial industry supported by men who might be squeamish about getting a flu shot but will happily permit their scalp to be removed in strips and replaced with skin from their necks. It's all because of the overpowering urge to copulate. The question arises: Did nature make a terrible mistake in our priorities—a simple error of design?

GENE: It wouldn't be the first.

GINA: It wouldn't?

GENE: I could cite many examples of bad design, from hiccups to eye boogers to the awkward geometry of the human buttock that creates the ridiculous need to "wipe," an incapacity otherwise unknown in the animal world. But nothing approaches the magnitude of the engineering error that nature blueprinted on men and that we must stoically bear. Mercedes-Benz technicians didn't accidentally make the front bumper out of Limoges china; no intelligent theory of design can explain why men must stride into each day preceded by their most vulnerable organs located *outside the body* in a little tulle-thin hackysack precisely at desktop-corner level.

GINA: You'll get no argument from me. Men are badly designed. A penis looks like a chicken neck that's been affixed with Elmer's Glue-All and is about to fall off.

GENE: Yes, penises are extremely silly-looking, unlike women's external genitalia, which are very dignified, and look nothing at all like a partially dissected squid.

This actually is an interesting point, designwise. The overpowering sexual urge is a form of slavish worship of the two most comical portions of the human anatomy. Still, the whole thing seems logical, in a heartless, theater-of-nature sort of way. Biologically speaking, the drive to reproduce is fanatically strong in all species. Animals will do astounding things to procreate. In 2003, scientists reported that the male southern elephant seal will roam as far as five thousand miles through the icy waters of Antarctica to mate.

GINA: Why do they have to travel so far to find a girl?

GENE: Here is a picture of the male southern elephant seal.

PHOTO BY A. RUS HOELZEL

GINA: You can't scare me—I've worked with guys like that. Is this going to be the only photograph in our book?

GENE: Yes.

GINA: Okay by me.

GENE: My point is that, as far as nature is concerned, all species—large or small, handsome or homuncular—have only one function: reproduction. As far as nature is concerned, the president pro tempore of the United States Senate is no more viable an organism than a stinkbug. The drive to reproduce overwhelms all else.

GINA: But male and female stinkbugs aren't always getting into embarrassing fights in front of the larvae. There's something about the nature of intelligence that creates this problem. We have the ability to overthink, so we do. Sex looms too large. We invest too much time worrying and planning. By the time we're old enough to experience it, we are already terrified of it.

GENE: I knew intense fear almost from day one. I was still very little when my mother explained to me how one goes about making a baby. She was a biology teacher, and her lesson was clinically excellent, but she neglected to mention a key point.

GINA: She didn't tell you it was fun.

GENE: Exactly!

GINA: Mothers never do. It's an awkward thing, explaining that the disgusting process you've just described makes Mommy and Daddy ever so happy.

GENE: Consequently, I was terrified that I would someday have to perform this terrible, revolting act, accidentally puke on "someone I loved very, very, much," and ruin everything. Later, when I began to strongly sense that this process might possibly be enjoyable, a new fear reared its ugly head, along with my first erection.

Erections in a twelve-year-old boy are an unstoppable and uncontrollable force of nature that can occur at any time—such as on the bus—and for no greater reason than that the boy might be thinking about the possibility, at some point in the future, of reflecting on the question of whether those Catholic-school girls' underpants are *also* plaid. And now—"Oh, shit, it's my stop." So for years my main fear about sex was that for the remainder of my adult life I would basically have to carry concealing objects at unnatural angles to avoid humiliation. I wondered how the president of the United States managed it.

Around this time I saw Buddy Hackett do a bit on TV in which he described a dinner date that went horribly wrong. Since the woman was beautiful and he was a gnome, Buddy felt he needed to marshal whatever meager resources he had. So he decided to demonstrate to her that he was sensitive, because women like that sort of thing. The best way to do that, he figured, was to shed a tear. To make that happen, he decided to surreptitiously yank out one of his nose hairs. Unfortunately, when he did, he got a nosebleed. This required him to cauterize the wound, using the candle at the table. But in so doing, he accidentally set his hair on fire, which forced him to extinguish the flames by pouring the bottle of champagne on his head, at which point his date ran away.

The audience was laughing uproariously, and so was I, but my laughter was hollow. I could easily see something like this happening to *me* one day. The vague fear of sex became coupled with the concrete fear of social ineptitude. Even before I had kissed any girls, they brought stark terror to my heart.

GINA: Sex scares girls, too. At a preteen slumber party, one of my girlfriends produced a condom she had stolen from her older brother's dresser drawer. We examined the evidence, trying to extrapolate from this object the dimensions of the male organ. (Available textbooks were disappointingly unclear.) The condom itself wasn't much help: As with pantyhose out of the L'Eggs container, we figured this thing would look entirely different when occupied.

So we decided to conduct a scientific experiment. We filled the condom with water, from the tap. When we were done we had something about a foot long and three inches in diameter. It weighed as much as an adult schnauzer. We sat there, awed, trying to imagine what such a thing would do to your internal organs. My friend Annemarie just sat in the corner and wept.

GENE: So maybe the solution to ending the gender wars is to institute very early, very explicit sex education that eliminates all fear, all uncertainty, and all mystery about the process.

GINA: It's happening already. Children's books today are very explicit and even emphasize the pleasure of the orgasm. They compare it to the sense of release you feel when you sneeze. Then it's all supplemented by a *fabulously* graphic full-color study guide, available far and wide at your finest porn sites everywhere.

GENE: True. And?

GINA: And it may be working, if the goal is to turn sex into a pleasurable but meaningless act, incidental to human relations, largely unconnected to love and commitment. Have you ever heard of a "fuck buddy"?

GENE: No.

GINA: You will. It's a term my college students use. It's common and getting commoner. A fuck buddy is someone in whom you are not romantically interested but with whom you regularly have intercourse. It's a service relationship, the equivalent of a lab partner or a member of your car pool. An alternative term for a fuck buddy is a "friend with benefits." I kid you not.

GENE: Okay. So what does this do to the gender war?

GINA: Well, by our theory, it disappears. Love still exists, and so does commitment, but because sex now has diminished mystery, it carries much less baggage and no longer becomes a tool of petty manipulation.

GENE: Hmm. No gender war.

GINA: Theoretically.

GENE: Do you buy this?

GINA: Not in the least.

GENE: Why?

GINA: Because I think that in the end, we actually *seek* sexual tension. It may be infuriating, but ultimately it's exciting. It's about the exercise of power, and that fascinates us. I think that if faced with a less passionate alternative, people will choose this grotesque dance we're in.

I think we're going to keep the status quo. I think that so long as there are men and women, whenever they engage each other in some way, there is going to be at least a small erotic component to the interaction. And so long as there is a theoretical potential for sexual congress, even if it is one that will never be realized, there is an undercurrent of sexual tension.

GENE: Any man and any woman?

GINA: I would say so. So long as they are engaging each other in some way.

GENE: Really?

GINA: It is seldom acknowledged or articulated—it can just sort of hang pregnant in the air—but I think it is always there.

GENE:

GINA: Do you disagree?

GENE: No, actually I don't.

GINA: See? We agree on something.

GENE: Yes, we do.

9

The Body Impolitic

GINA: I propose that we explore a question that is seldom confronted openly, even though it is symptomatic of the continuing oppression of women in our society, and central to the gulf that divides the sexes. Ready?

GENE: Shoot.

GINA: Why don't men like fat women?

GENE: Don't shoot.

GINA: What?

GENE: This is not a question I want to tackle.

GINA: Why?

GENE: Because it infuriates people. Over the years in my humor column I have gleefully poked fun at taboo subjects such as religion and ethnicity, with few complaints. I have made light of disease and dying, age and senescence, and have gotten mostly laughs. But whenever I have suggested ever so gently that there might be something amusing about a human the size of a convenience store, readers are appalled. Letters are written.

Subscriptions are canceled. For some reason, the complaints are always from women.

GINA: That's because men assume you're talking about someone else. A woman thinks she's fat if she can't still fit into a size ten. A man thinks he's fat if he can't still fit into a foreign sports car. There are rules for body image, and they've been set by men.

In the early 1990s, behavioral researchers in Canada planted two bogus personal ads in a newspaper. The ads were almost identical, except in one, the woman was described as "a recovering addict with eleven months of sobriety," and in the other she was described as "fifty pounds overweight." Four times as many men responded to Cokie than to Chubby.

The issue of weight creates a serious rupture in the male/female dynamic. It's unfair, it's hurtful to women, and I want to discuss it.

GENE: Couldn't we discuss something a little less controversial, such as abortion?

GINA: Fat. We are discussing fat. It's important.

Fear of fat incapacitates women. The very publication of the word causes women to put down whatever they are reading and back up toward the nearest mirror in that sidelong way that permits you to approach the image of your behind slowly, not getting the whole thing in focus at once, so that you can look away if the experience threatens to becomes too intense. The actual inspection is conducted through half-closed eyes, which is the equivalent of watching a scary movie between your slitted fingers. This is going on right now in homes and libraries and bookstores across the country as women read this page. It must stop. We are going to discuss it. Don't be such a coward.

GENE: Okay. Just don't give me the Marilyn thing.

GINA: What Marilyn thing?

GENE: Every time I write about weight, I get dozens of letters from indignant women who would have me know, buster, that Marilyn Monroe wore a size sixteen.

GINA: She did.

GENE: Oh, for crying out loud. It's an urban myth.

GINA: If it is, it's amazingly enduring. It's been a part of feminist dialogue for years. Marilyn was a big girl—sexy, alluring, and comfortable with her size. Which was a sixteen.

GENE: I can see why feminists would not wish to subject this little nugget of misinformation to the most rigorous scrutiny, but suffice it to say that if Marilyn Monroe were standing next to a woman of equal height who wore a size sixteen, they would form the number 80. Marilyn was five feet five and a half inches tall. To be a modern size sixteen she would have had to weigh at least 170 pounds.

GINA: And you know this because you are an expert on women's sizes?

GENE: I am not. I know nothing about women's sizes.

GINA: Well, then.

GENE: Fortunately, Thea *is* an expert on women's sizes. She is a saleswoman at Ann Taylor in Washington, D.C., and I have her on the phone right now. Thea, if a woman were five feet five and a half inches tall and wore a size sixteen, how much would she weigh?

THEA: One seventy to 180.

GENE: Thank you.

THEA: You're welcome.

GINA: I fail to see what that proves. Marilyn might have been that size. She was hardly petite. Forty years after her death, her weight would be impossible to prove one way or another.

THOMAS NOGUCHI: Actually, that's not true.

GINA: Who are you?

GENE: Dr. Noguchi is the famous Los Angeles coroner who performed Marilyn's autopsy. I invited him here. Doctor, could you please tell us what your scales revealed Ms. Monroe's naked body to weigh at the time of her death, on August 4, 1962, at the age of thirty-six?

DR. NOGUCHI: One hundred seventeen pounds.

GENE: And are you confident these scales were accurate? Could they have been in error by, oh, say . . . fifty pounds or so?

DR. NOGUCHI: Weighing people's remains is a serious business. We use a body scale. We weigh the body on a gurney and then subtract the weight of the gurney. It's not an estimate, it's exact.

GENE: Thank you, Doctor. I appreciate your stopping by.

GINA:

GENE: I rest my case.

GINA: As far as I am concerned, that only proves that death is the ultimate diet.

GENE: Nice try.

GINA: Since you dragged in Marilyn, you will not object if I drag in my own celebrities?

GENE: Be my guest.

GINA: Why is George Wendt, the tub of pudding who played Norm on *Cheers,* married to a cute little thing, while women of size cannot get dates? Why is this phenomenon so common? Why does the guy who played Newman on *Seinfeld* land his perky, huge-bosomed makeup artist? Why is Mrs. John Goodman a pleasantly proportioned woman fifteen years her husband's junior?

GENE: Because those guys' wallets are also fat?

GINA: But rich, fat *women* aren't married to young studs. No, the explanation for the Goodman and Wendt and Newman nuptials is that women see beyond looks. Did you ever wonder why it is mostly straight women and gay men who like to shop for nice clothes, get their hair done, use skin cream, and so forth? The reason is that straight women and gay men are both trying to attract *men,* and they know that *men,* being shallow, care inordinately about looks. Lesbians, on the other hand, wear message T-shirts and cargo pants and keep their hair "easy to manage." This is because lesbians are looking to attract *women*, who are not shallow. They care about the important things.

GENE: So, basically, you contend that when men are not in the picture, women are realistic—totally free of self-deception and irrational concerns for style over substance and appearance over reality. As opposed to men.

GINA: Yes.

GENE: Then explain this, please. A store specializing in clothing for fat men will be named something like the Big, Husky & Huge Flabby Guy's Clothes Warehouse. But a store specializing in clothing for fat women will be named something like Jacqueline Depardieux, Ltd. In the guy's store, reasonably, as you get fatter your size gets bigger. A guy who is five feet ten and weighs 320 pounds knows what he is. He is a size sixty-six. But in Jacqueline Depardieux, Ltd., there *are no* huge sizes. As you get fatter, your sizes go up, until they start getting smaller again!

GINA: They're called plus sizes. They are a euphemism. But this is because our male-dominated society has poisoned women into being defensive about their body shape.

GENE: Women's fashions are *drowning* in euphemism. Case in point: My wife is either a size two or a size four. She's tiny. So when I went to buy her a shirt for Christmas a couple years ago, I picked out a nice size three, figuring I would split the difference. So she opens the present and bursts out laughing. Holds it up like a matador's cape. I admit that—in the extreme tension of shopping for women's clothes in the accepted male manner of trying to get in and out as quickly as possible—I had not noticed that the shirt I had bought was large enough to be a tea cozy for a garbage can. It was a size three, but there was an *X* after the number.

"Where did you *get* this?" my wife asked, stifling a grin.

"Hecht's," I said.

"Where in Hecht's?" she interrogated. (She is a federal prosecutor.)

"The women's department," I said.

"Hahahaha," my wife said. My daughter, a college student, also thought this a total hoot.

What a jerk I had been! In looking for a garment for a woman, I stupidly went to a department designated for . . . women. Any *fool* would have known that in the highly straightforward, completely realistic world of women selling to women, *misses* means "women," and *women* means "fat women."

GINA: You are exhibiting all the sensitivity of a burlap condom.

GENE: This was your idea, missy.

GINA: That does not excuse a "tea cozy for a garbage can."

GENE: Gina?

GINA: What?

GENE: I want to ask you something, but I don't know how.

GINA: I can help. You don't know for sure what I look like. And because I am passionate on this subject, you think I must be overweight. So you want to ask me if I am.

GENE: Yes.

GINA: What if I told you that I weighed 413 pounds? Would you like me less? Would we still be engaged in this extensive, elaborate flirtation?

GENE:

GINA: Your ineloquence speaks with astonishing eloquence.

GENE: A man likes to be able to get his arms around a woman.

GINA: Why?

GENE: I don't know.

GINA: Yes, you do. It is because men are intimidated by women, so the less of us, the better. Through most of our country's history, American men have encouraged women to look as weak and helpless as possible. Scarlett O'Hara feared working outdoors because a tan would betray the unfeminine fact that she had to work.

March forward fifty years. Women in early-twentieth-century New York *wanted* tans, because it was a sign that they didn't work indoors, in the factories. In both cases, femininity was defined as uselessness, even weakness. American furniture makers once marketed "swooning couches" for women, who were built like tweezers, to sink into with "the vapors." The fact is, this is unnatural. It runs counter to Darwin. If a cavewoman swooned, she got eaten. And I don't mean that in a *good* way.

GENE: So is there such a thing as being too fat?

GINA: You are too fat if your husband doesn't walk next to you, but walks among you. You are too fat if you need a winch to get into a room.

GENE: That was insensitive to winch-dependent people.

GINA: I'll risk the letters.

GENE: You're not 413 pounds, are you?

GINA: Bothered by this, are we?

GENE: No.

GINA: Then the answer is immaterial.

GENE: That number you came up with was very specific.

GINA: Yes, it was.

GENE:

GINA: Let me ask this. If I were 413 pounds, could you have a romantic interest in me? Tell me the truth, and I'll tell you the truth.

GENE: The truth is yes, I could.

GINA: Perhaps I have misjudged you. No, I am not 413 pounds. I am short and a little round. When I wear white I can be mistaken for a wheel of Brie. But I am considered cute by men who discriminate. So, you weren't lying? You really could have a romantic interest in me at 413 pounds?

GENE: Sure. If you were nine feet tall.

GINA: Asshole.

10

Why Do Fowls Fall in Love?
(A Treatise on Desire)

GINA: Fowls?

GENE: Right.

GINA: We are examining the love life of poultry?

GENE: As a starting point of inquiry. Animals often offer an accurate, if primitive, template for human behavior.

GINA: Except chickens don't fall in love.

GENE: Exactly. Animals don't go all gooey for their sex partners. Dogs will fall madly in love, but only with their owners. That's different. It's pragmatic. It ensures their survival by provoking a corresponding love in the humans who control their lives. But *sexually* speaking, a dog will happily find romance by fornicating with some bitch in heat behind a Dumpster. Parrots, wolves, and geese sometimes mate for life, but they're notable as exceptions. Yet all species survive. So if romantic love isn't genetically necessary, why does it happen to us?

GINA: I'm not sure it isn't genetically necessary. Love is basically an intense partnership cemented in mutual need. Cave-

people probably knew something like love. Another body tucked close kept you warm at night, and if you slept back to back, it kept you safer, too. All eyes were facing danger—you literally had each other's back. That meant there was less of a chance a wild boar would rip out your kidney, except for the perilous but necessary three and a half seconds for coitus. Come to think of it, that probably explains why men are always done so fast.

GENE: You seem to have a thing about premature ejaculation.

GINA: All women have a thing about premature ejaculation.

GENE: So are you saying that love is vestigial—imprinted in our genes but of no value in a civilized word without marauding boars?

GINA: Possibly. I've heard it argued that love helps us stay together so as to better raise and protect our children, but even Darwinian scholars don't put much stock in that. The desired result, adaptively, seems to be protection of the baby, not protection of the union. And scientists believe protection of the baby is primarily encouraged through the kid's helpless and cute appearance.

A fascinating 1995 study actually suggests that babies tend to resemble their fathers more than their mothers, which—considering male egotism—encourages the dad to stick around. Evolutionarily, love for self trumps love for wife.

As to why adults fall in love with each other, science mostly fails us. We have only anecdotal evidence. Why did you fall in love with your wife?

GENE: Early in our courtship, before she went to law school, she was considering becoming a police officer. She aced the written test, but then she had to take a physical exam that would require her to carry eighty pounds of dead weight on her back, to prove she could rescue an unconscious person. She barely weighed that much herself and had no idea if she could do it. So she went to the supermarket, bought two forty-pound sacks of Kibbles 'n Bits, duct-taped them together, and practiced lugging them around the house. When I saw that, she had me.

GINA: That was actually the moment?

GENE: I remember it like yesterday.

GINA: I think you're on to something. Being people is more complicated than being poultry. Your point is that we fall in love because we subconsciously recognize in another person those characteristics we need to complement and reinforce our own strengths and which therefore better adapt us, as a team, to face the hardships of life. In your wife's case, these qualities— exemplified by the dog food—were perseverance, practicality, resourcefulness, the determination to transcend physical limitations, and, probably most significant to you, the willingness to sacrifice dignity in the pursuit of a more important ideal.

What you're saying is that once we have intellectually found an evolutionarily suitable partner, nature supplies love as a sort of dowry, a little bribe to further encourage the match.

GENE: I just thought the whole thing accentuated her excellent behind.

GINA: You are simply translating what I said into Manspeak. Manspeak is mostly grunts. Your theory isn't far removed from some religious explanations. Both the Talmud and the Rosicrucian Kabbalah, for example, contend that men and women were each created lacking something that is present only in the other, and that in falling in love we find what is missing and become one with ourselves.

GENE: I like the dog food theory better.

GINA: So do I. I refuse to believe that everything goes back to that dippy old Melanie lyric, "I've got a brand-new pair of roller skates, you've got a brand-new key." There's an unattractive New Age-y narcissism to defining love strictly in terms of what it does for you. It's just a quick skip-step from that to blaming whatever is missing in your life on someone else. Contemporary women reject that.

GENE: So, basically, you're saying that I am a feminist philosopher, a hero to your gender.

GINA: Basically, I am saying that I am excited by this because it supports La Rochefoucauld, who is never wrong. La Rochefoucauld said, "If no one had learned to read, very few people would be in love."

GENE: What the hell does that mean?

GINA: It means that romantic love is natural but not instinctive, as is love for one's child. Romantic love as we practice it today is a more sophisticated phenomenon, an acquired taste that requires a degree of refinement and experience. You have to be familiar with something to desire it. A Bedouin tribesman does not wake up one day and say, out of the blue, "You know what I would really like? I would really like a milk chocolate bonbon with a chewy nougat center." I love La Rochefoucauld.

GENE: You love him?

GINA: It's a different sort of love, but equally refined. He also said, "Old people are fond of giving good advice; it consoles them for no longer being capable of setting a bad example."

GENE: What does that have to do with anything?

GINA: I will happily quote La Rochefoucauld out of context. Love blinds a woman to small imperfections.

The fact is, in analyzing love, he was observing something

borne out by history: Romance as we understand it today is a surprisingly recent phenomenon. I am talking about the notion that a man and a woman who are intoxicated by love for each other decide to commit to a lifelong relationship, one that is driven by passion and mutual respect and caring, and sanctioned as a good and wholesome thing both by God and by secular society. Very recent.

Whatever impulse toward love that may have been kindled in those Pleistocene caves was systematically beaten out of us and suppressed over the years as civilization thudded forward and the custodians of public conduct laid down restrictive rules. Love as we understand it today wasn't really sanctioned. The most celebrated love stories of the last millennium are actually stories of astonishing dysfunction.

Remember Héloïse and Abelard? Outside of fiction, it's probably the most famous love story of all time. Pierre Abelard was a twelfth-century French theologian. He was charged with tutoring the seventeen-year-old beauty Héloïse in the ways of God. Instead, the two fell head over heels for each other. Literally. Many furtive gropings ensued, and a baby was produced. They married in secret. The Roman Catholic Church was not amused, and Church elders exacted their punishment.

GENE: I know this story. It is painful and uncomfortable and I do not like it.

GINA: You seem to have a thing about castration.

GENE: All men have a thing about castration.

GINA: Abelard was left to live the rest of his life, alone, emasculated, worshiping God and contemplating his grievous sin: love. The Roman Catholic Church was quite clear on this, and Abelard came to believe the Church was right.

GENE: And Héloïse was condemned to wander through history, a pitiable Zelig-like creature yammering on to newspaper readers everywhere with helpful hints about how to make a used doily into a snood.

GINA: Actually, the historical Héloïse showed a lot more gumption than Abelard. She spent the rest of her life cloistered and bitter, cursing the Church. The point is, the story survived as a parable about the folly of the flesh. At the dawning of the last millennium and well on into it, feeling intensely for another human being, even one's spouse, was considered a human frailty. It was a betrayal of God, for whom one's love had to be pure and perfect and in competition with nothing earthly. Marriage existed largely for the banal purpose of procreation.

GENE: That's harsh.

GINA: They were harsh times. For centuries afterward, even once romantic love was recognized as something that could befall the virtuous, it was permissible only in a sort of stylized and theoretical way. You've heard of the great love story of Dante Alighieri and Beatrice Portinari?

GENE: I have.

GINA: How many times do you think they did it?

GENE: I don't know.

GINA: Guess.

GENE: Twelve.

GINA: How did you come up with that?

GENE: It's the funniest-sounding number.

GINA: "Umpteen" is the funniest-sounding number.

GENE: That's made up. Twelve is *naturally* funny. You just have to say it out loud, and you laugh.

The Twelve is a bird with a hairy caboose
That dwells in the land of the good Doctor Seuss.

GINA: Are we through with this?

GENE: Okay. How many times did Dante and Beatrice do it?

GINA: Zero. Dante and his beloved Beatrice didn't really ever meet. Dante spotted Beatrice only from afar, once as a child, once as an adolescent, and a few more times as an adult, for what appears to be a total of about six minutes. He decided she was the most desirable human on the planet and, accordingly, was paralyzed into nerdlike stammering in her presence.

By never acting on his carnal desire, he never got to know Beatrice. He never saw her cutting her toenails or using a pumice stone on her calluses. His passion was unsullied by reality. Beatrice became not his wife but his muse. His torment over this unrequited love informed some of his greatest works, including his portrayal of the Stygian depths of hell.

By comparison, Shakespeare gave Romeo and Juliet—the most famous love story of all time—a much more active sex life. They actually got to spend a single night together in sexual congress, prior to burbling to death side by side in a dank catacomb. You see where we are going here?

GENE: You're showing off?

GINA: I am making the point that these pathetic nonrelationships are the enduring *great love stories of Western civilization*. For most of recorded time, passionate, romantic love was seen as a heretical act—forbidden to most of us, punished when it occurred. In the classic stories that endure—both true ones and those idealized as fiction—love is torment, essentially an insanity. The consequences are dire. When Lancelot stopped pining platonically for Guinevere and actually bedded her, the ensuing scandal helped bring down Camelot.

This was no accident. For much of recorded history, life was nasty and brutish and short—you know, like most of the guys we date. Those in power needed to keep people in line and reasonably satisfied in their misery, and the way to do that was to promise a heavenly reward for earthly suffering.

The word *heretic* comes from the Greek, meaning "one who chooses." Choice was bad. It was essential to the Church, and to the nobility, that the rabble be contained—because if the rabble made choices in love, they might make other choices about what they did with their time. They might decide they wanted to be a wheelwright, for example, instead of being the eighth generation of their family to dig turnips for the lord of the manor.

The point is, one was supposed to repress desire: desire for education, desire for material wealth, and, you know, desire. Period.

GENE: When did it become okay to act on love and mold your life around it?

GINA: Much later than you'd guess. Here's another great love story: In 1817, England's Duke of Kent was faced with a challenge. His country wanted him to stop living in sin with his French paramour, whom he deeply loved, and marry a woman whom he didn't, in order to produce a proper heir to the British throne. What do you think he did?

GENE: Not sure.

GINA: There was also a rather large financial incentive.

GENE: He did it.

GINA: Yes, he did. Never saw his beloved again. His marriage was hailed as a great act of a great man, placing country above heart. Interestingly, the marriage produced only one child, a sturdy baby girl. Her name was Victoria, and she presided over a century celebrated for its prudish restraint of desire.

When desire finally was permitted to erupt, it was still misshapen. In 1911, Freud published something called *The Most Prevalent Form of Degradation in Erotic Life,* in which he pointed out that the typical man finds it almost impossible to feel love and sexual desire for the same woman. If he loves her, he can't desire her, and if he desires her, he can't love her. It was the mistress phenomenon, the one that creates a society in which it is customary for men to be promiscuous and for women to be chaste. Every man wants to be a woman's first love, and every woman wants to be a man's last love.

GENE: You sound ridiculously positive about all this.

GINA: This is the magic of academia. Flat pronouncements are accepted. For example, I am prepared to flatly declare the date upon which all of this began to change.

GENE: A single date?

GINA: Yes. It was January 10, 1931. It was a Saturday. It was raining. Are you going to challenge me?

GENE: Nope.

GINA: Of course not. I have a Ph.D. in this stuff. On that day, England's Prince of Wales, heir apparent to the British throne, was at a London cocktail party hosted by Lady Furness. Across the room he spied a hot little flat-chested American number, accompanied by her husband. It was much the way Dante first spied Beatrice—only Edward was no tongue-tied geek. It took him a while, but eventually he pounced.

And, interestingly, times had changed. Everyone and everything fell into line; even Mrs. Simpson's husband did the right proper thing and stepped nobly aside. By subsequently renouncing his throne for the woman he loved, Edward VIII turned the whole Duke of Kent precedent on its head—he placed heart above country, and for this decision he was celebrated the world over.

GENE: And now?

GINA: And now one is *expected* to order one's life around the tug of one's heart. Unfortunately, the echoes of the past still remain. The great love stories resonate, particularly with women. Romance is still inextricably associated with pain and torment, and the myth persists that if you are not miserable, you are not really in love. This has placed a double whammy on modern women: You are expected to give up everything for love, *and* it is supposed to hurt.

It explains why, to this day, so many young women are not attracted to nice guys who want to love them always and encourage them in their ambitions and respect their talents and anticipate their needs and forgive their shortcomings and remain single-mindedly devoted to their happiness. They are going to be attracted to the guy in the ribbed T-shirt with the one headlight out on his car.

GENE: And this is the fault of men?

GINA: No. It is the fault of women. We are responsible for our own decisions and their consequences.

GENE:

GINA: What?

GENE: I'm waiting for the uncontrollable spasm of shrill, self-pitying, phallophobic blame flinging.

GINA: There will be none. Feminists are quite clear on this matter.

GENE:

GINA: Even though the patterns of behavior leading to this situation *were* set in motion by centuries of oppression during which the rules for the conduct of intimacy were under the despotic control of men determined to preserve their power by stifling not only the will of the masses, but their very capacity to love and be spiritually fulfilled, a condition that still disproportionately reverberates in the emotional subjugation of women.

GENE: Thank you.

11

Marriage:
It Takes Two to Tangle

GENE: I recently ran into a friend of mine I hadn't seen since high school. I'll call him Fred. Fred told me a horror story to chill the blood of any man.

GINA: I don't like "Fred." Call him something else.

GENE: This is my anecdote. I can pick the name.

GINA: In choosing pseudonyms, it's important to communicate the correct feel for a person. "Fred" is a dorky name. It makes him sound stupid and clumsy. Is he stupid and clumsy?

GENE: He's a surgeon.

GINA: Well, then.

GENE: Fred Astaire wasn't stupid and clumsy.

GINA: Fred Astaire had the most inappropriate first name of any celebrity, ever. It's a wonder his career survived it.

GENE: No, "Gladys" Knight is worse. Also "Humphrey" Bogart and "Mel" Gibson.

GINA: Well, I think you should call your high-school friend "Maurice."

GENE: Gina?

GINA: What?

GENE: Why are we having this conversation?

GINA: Because of the subject of this chapter. We are cleverly making a point through role-playing.

GENE: We are?

GINA: Yes. Marriage is about negotiation and compromise. If it is Fred, my disappointment will register in the form of an inability to actively participate in this conversation. That would be a shame because I have many provocative and entertaining things to say.

GENE:

GINA: Marriage is also about power politics.

GENE: So I and Maurice—*whom I call Moe*—were catching each other up on the events of the last thirty-five years or so, which included, in his case, an unhappy marriage that ended in acrimonious divorce. When I asked him why he'd gotten married, Moe got a sheepish look on his face, took a huge swallow of beer, and explained.

One day, he and his college girlfriend had been enjoying each other's company in a manner consistent with the times—by which I mean hours of thrashing intercourse fueled by drink and dope and choreographed to throbbing acid rock. During an exhausted lull in these proceedings, informed by the sort of judgment and emotional insight that can only be delivered by near-fatal doses of recreational chemicals, Moe just sort of babbled out the idea that it might be groovy as all heck to get married.

"Then what happened?" I asked him.

Moe stared at his glass as though it were a tombstone. "She rolled off me," he said, "and called her mother."

GINA: Hahahaha.

GENE: So we just sat there for a while, my poor, sad old friend and I. Finally, he said: "Jewish girl." I just nodded.

GINA: An Italian girl would never have done that. An Italian girl would have boinked him again, *then* called her mother. But I don't see your point.

GENE: My point is an old one, first advanced by my favorite Greek philosopher, Anonymous: "Sex is the price women pay for marriage. Marriage is the price men pay for sex." A bad bit of commerce, in both directions.

GINA: You are taking a position in opposition to marriage?

GENE: I'm certainly taking a position in opposition to weddings. Moe's problem was not caused by marriage so much as it was caused by the sudden, startling appearance of an impending wedding. At the moment the phone call was made, the countdown to the wedding began, and that is a countdown accompanied by an inextinguishable fuse. He was screwed.

GINA: He certainly was.

GENE: See previous Greek quotation.

GINA: Point taken.

GENE: I oppose *everything* about weddings, which tend to be unattractive exercises in the celebration of self, entailing enormous costs that, even if affordable, would be far better donated to the newly married couple for the purposes of beginning a life together. Everything about the event is vulgar excess and ostentation, best exemplified by the fact that bridesmaids are compelled to purchase expensive, unnatural outfits in unappealing colors, outfits that can never be worn again because they look as though they were fashioned from motel draperies. This is all for use in an event involving logistics so bizarre, and so petty, that they can and sometimes do create lifetime enmities among otherwise reasonable people.

GINA: You are the father of a potential bride, are you not?

GENE: I am.

GINA: I see.

GENE: That's irrelevant. It's not just about money. It's about the fact that it's a celebration of a decision that's just not very important. Getting married, by itself, is a triviality.

GINA: Really?

GENE: I should explain that Gina's previous line was delivered in a tone of voice such that, were this not a book but a cartoon on the comics pages, the little word balloon would have been drawn with icicles dripping from it.

Yes, "really." Marriage, under most circumstances, is pretty pointless and silly.

GINA: Explain, then, why you married the dog food lady.

GENE: We got married for legal reasons, when we decided to have children after living together for years. Otherwise, it never would have happened.

GINA: I don't believe that.

GENE: We are not so childlike or insecure that we required a government and/or religious authority to officially certify that, as far as some deputy assistant secretary of public records is concerned, we love each other, intend to stay together indefinitely, and will not cheat on each other. We don't need a treaty to enforce it.

GINA: That's not why people get married. People get married to acknowledge to the world around them that they are a partnership and to certify that partnership in a formal way.

GENE: Love is about two people. You make a promise to the

other person, and if things work out well, you keep your promise. You try to keep that promise not because you've signed a contract, but because you owe it to each other. It is an entirely private matter. That is one reason I find the term "fiancée" so ludicrous.

GINA: What's wrong with "fiancée"?

GENE: Icicles again!

Apart from being French and therefore sounding ridiculously affected, the word serves no function other than explaining that this other person is someone I *plan* to marry at some point in the future. Why does a word have to exist to describe that tenuous status, which is no one's business anyway? Why not have a word to mean "the person whom I am *intending* to hire to paint my kitchen"?

GINA: You equate the two, do you?

GENE: Actually, the kitchen thing probably *does* require a contract. As I said, I think marriage is a private promise, a state of mind. It's only when kids arrive that suddenly your promise becomes much more solemn, because other lives are involved. Your responsibilities become exponentially greater, because your selfishness or irresponsible judgments can affect innocents. *That's* when there's a need for paperwork. Before that, you're just going steady.

GINA: You think that Michael and I, who have been married thirteen years but have no children, are just "going steady"?

GENE: It's nothing to be ashamed of. He's obviously a fabulous date.

GINA: Don't be an ass. Marriage is an entirely different thing, an entirely different state of being. It's like the difference between owning a house and renting. It's a matter of permanence, as much a mind-set as anything else. When my friend Pam was renting apartments in New York City, she never defrosted a freezer. When the freezer needed defrosting, she'd move. Do you see my point?

GENE: Yes. Your point needs defrosting. I think a romantic relationship—absent children—is about trust, not legal responsibility.

GINA: It's trust underwritten by legal responsibility.

GENE: So you need an underwriter? How about throwing in an actuary and a certified public accountant? Isn't it odd that I have the more romantic view of this?

GINA: You don't. Your view of marriage seems to require the taking of hostages.

GENE: Yours requires payment schedules. Delinquent notices. Collateral.

GINA: Men can be such hypocrites.

GENE: You are calling me a hypocrite?

GINA: I am. Ordinarily, you guys love contracts. Men will write a sports contract stipulating how many bars of soap a middle linebacker will get in the locker room. Men *invented* contracts. When the issue was divvying up the power to loot and sack and oppress the masses, men wrote the Magna Carta. But when the issue involves contributing to the security of a woman, they get all squishy and romantic. Contracts about relationships become gauche.

GENE: From a practical standpoint, all the modern marriage contract supplies is some sort of government imprimatur on our basest impulses toward possessiveness and jealousy. Marriage should not be about possessiveness and jealousy.

GINA: Yes, it should be. It should be a great big pasta dish called possessiveness, and it is best when liberally seasoned with jealousy. Jealousy is the sweet basil of emotions. La Rochefoucauld wrote, "Jealousy is in some measure just and reasonable, since it merely aims at keeping something that belongs to us, or we think belongs to us, whereas envy is a frenzy that cannot bear anything that belongs to others."

GENE: That's really pretty with faeries dancing on it. I'm beginning to dislike that guy.

GINA: Getting jealous, are we? It's good for you. It's even natural. It's Darwinian.

GENE: Jealousy is Darwinian?

GINA: As Darwinian as the desire for sex. A University of New Mexico study concluded that women who are ovulating get horny for men other than their husbands or partners. It seems counterintuitive, doesn't it? You'd think that for the sake of home and hearth and the survival of the species, the women would clamp right onto their husband-partners, like a remora on a shark.

But here is what is interesting: Nature corrects for that. The study also found that when these women were looking around with frank interest elsewhere, their own men sensed this and moved in on them to monopolize their time. Jealousy compelled them to stop taking their women for granted. Jealousy is an evolutionary adaptation, a tool for good.

GENE: By that argument, my marriage should have ended twenty years ago. I am married to the least jealous woman on earth.

GINA: All women are jealous.

GENE: Not my wife. Possibly it is because she resembles Martha Stewart and I resemble a sebaceous cyst with ears.

GINA: Makes no difference. Jealousy takes no notice of looks or logic. There are no exceptions.

GENE: There's at least one.

GINA: I doubt it.

GENE: A few years ago I went to Miami with my editor, Rich, to a convention of journalists. We'd been asked to deliver a presentation about the editor-writer relationship. We wrote the speech on the airplane. As one part of our shtick, playing the role of an obnoxious, imperious editor, I was to command Rich to put on a brassiere, and Rich (in the role of a docile writer) would comply.

So when we got to Miami, we stopped in a department store and purchased a bra that would fit over Rich and his clothing—which is to say, a huge one. I think it was a 44DD. We gave the presentation and then came home. Several days passed. And suddenly I woke from a deep sleep with a horrible realization: When we left Miami, I had simply stashed the bra in my suitcase with my dirty clothes. And my wife had unpacked the suitcase and done the laundry. It was 3 A.M. I woke her up.

"Um, honey, did you notice anything unusual in the laundry?"

She said, "Wha, uh, the bra?"

I said, "Yeah. Isn't there anything you want to know?"

She said, "I just figured you'd have some stupid explanation." And without even waiting for an answer, she turned over and went back to sleep.

GINA: If you were my husband, following that little episode—had I even chosen to interrogate you before staving out your heart with a trowel—you would have had to start carrying a spy-cam on your belt at all times.

I love my husband and trust him implicitly, until such time as I have a real reason for suspicion, such as whenever he is in physical proximity to a woman under fifty. And that age will increase over time.

Sometimes people will ask me why so many of my girlfriends are lesbians. I tell them that this way I know my friends are not hitting on my husband.

GENE: Is he allowed to be alone with his female students?

GINA: Certainly. What do you think I am, a crackpot?

GENE: No, but—

GINA: He just has to keep the office door open a little.

GENE: Are you kidding?

GINA: Only slightly. Listen, I am a middle-aged woman in her second marriage. It is to a middle-aged man in his second marriage, and this is a marriage I value highly. Moreover, I am an Italian-American. I am not without passion and I am not slow to anger. The extreme pleasure of my company comes at a small price.

GENE: One's freedom?

GINA: One's freedom to cheat. Isn't there a price *you* pay for the, shall we say, somnolent calm in your marriage?

GENE: It isn't calmness. It's security.

GINA: They can be synonymous. Jealousy is part of passion. I'm sure you love each other. But I'm seriously wondering if you remain *in* love.

GENE: Whoa.

GINA: You started this.

GENE: My wife is a lawyer with grave responsibilities. She is very much the adult of our marriage. Well, the other day we were in the car, talking about something serious—I believe it was the brinkmanship of the Bush administration's foreign policy—when that dweeby '60s song "Good Morning Starshine" came on the radio. Without breaking cadence, my wife elided straight from one foreign-policy sentence into the song's refrain, which she nailed, singing along syllable for syllable without a misstep. I'd like to quote the lyrics here, but when I asked EMI Music for permission, they demanded to first see the actual page on which the lyrics would appear, in context. I realized this was doomed, inasmuch as the context was that I was going to call "Good Morning Starshine" a song written by weenies for the entertainment of dipshits. So I withdrew the request, and now cannot print the lyrics without getting sued. But I think you know them. They sound exactly like this:

> Gloopy boop schmoopie, sippy sappy soupie
> Tra la la whoa whoa.
> Yadda wadda shmata, boopsie olly wally
> Lay low yo yo.
> Whoopsie oopsie whoppa, scoopy moopy poppa
> Early mornin' sippin' song . . .

My wife went right through to the unforgettable hook line, "Sing a song, song a sing," and then returned to foreign affairs, midsentence, on message.

I am in awe of the dog food lady. Yes, I remain in love.

GINA: That was so sweet.

GENE: Whatever.

GINA: No, I mean it. I'm sorry we had a fight.

GENE: We had a fight?

GINA: We said hurtful things to each other.

GENE: We did?

GINA: Yes. I'm sorry.

GENE: No problem.

GINA: I say "I'm sorry," and you say "No problem"?

GENE: What am I supposed to say?

GINA: Think real hard.

GENE: I'm sorry, too?

GINA: Good. Now remove the question mark.

GENE: I'm sorry, too!

GINA: Excellent.

GENE: I didn't even know we'd had a fight.

GINA: Men seldom do. They need to be instructed when to be contrite. Fortunately, they usually are pretty docile about that part of it.

GENE: That's because we know the penalty for resistance is far greater than the pain of compliance. The truth is, we don't really mind losing an argument. We don't keep score.

GINA: Women do.

GENE: I know.

GINA: You're behind 73–6.

Gina's Guide for Men: How to Know When You Are Having a Fight

The Clue	Its Meaning
A sudden, startling increase in conversational politeness.	"We are strangers. I do not really know you because the man I married could not possibly have behaved in such a repugnant fashion. We are starting all over again, until such time as you convince me through your actions that your *previous* actions were a momentary lapse in judgment that you sincerely regret."

Very. Short. Answers.

"Because of your inconsiderate behavior, it is apparent you are no longer interested, *if you ever were,* in my view of things. And so I shall not irritate or bore you with any words other than the minimum required to respond to your inquiries, such as "yes," "no," and the icy "oh?" This monosyllabic lexicon will be broken only when it becomes necessary to express my acceptance of an apology, possibly accompanied by a gift, and I do not mean lingerie or costume jewelry but something that demonstrates what your actions suggest you do not have, namely, a familiarity with those things that bring me pleasure."

Unnecessarily loud physical actions

"Inasmuch as your selfish conduct suggests that you have forgotten that you reside in this house with another human being, I shall endeavor to remind you of this by, for example, placing dishes on the kitchen shelves as though they were cymbals crashing during the third movement of Tchaikovsky's *Pathétique.* These sounds will pursue you in various forms as you move from room to room in a correspondingly pathetic and futile effort to re-move yourself from the source of irritation in much the same way you have cho-sen to remove yourself emo-tionally from each and every situation calling for tender-ness or authenticity, which happens to be the precise dysfunction that is the cause of your current punishment."

Lack of eye contact.

"For reasons legal and practi-cal, it is impossible at the moment for me to move out of the house so as to spare myself the agony of sharing it with a person as malignant as yourself. Perhaps it will seem as though you are not there if I simply fail to see you."

Gene's Guide for Women: How to Interpret Men's Behavior After a Fight

The Action	Its Meaning
He sincerely begs your forgiveness.	He does not know what he has done wrong, but he loves you.
He buys you a present.	He does not know what he has done wrong, but he loves you and wants to have sex.
He buys you a really expensive present.	He does not know what he has done wrong, but he loves you and wants to have sex, including that thing you sometimes do to him. You know, that thing. That special thing.
He takes you someplace really, really romantic—like that little restaurant where he proposed.	He kind of suspects what he has done wrong. And it isn't good.
He leaps out the window.	All things considered, it's just easier.

12

Infidelity:
Get Out Your Hanky.
And Your Panky.

GENE: Marital infidelity. Funny or not?

GINA: Not.

GENE: I disagree. Stealth is funny. Stealth in the service of the gratification of oneself is very funny. Hypocrisy in connection with stealth in the service of the gratification of oneself is hilarious. For example, when some years ago the aptly named Senator Robert "Packwood" was revealed to be an indefatigable, chase-around-the-desk, pin-against-the-wall kissyface bandit, there was a great deal of solemn tsking from many other aptly named "members" of Congress, who were shocked—*shocked*—that a married man could behave in such a way. When the Lewinsky scandal broke, the tsk choir achieved philharmonic proportions.

It was as though history has not amply shown us that, left to their own devices, married men—in particular, powerful married men—tend to be as trustworthy as those bargain-priced cellophane-thin kitchen garbage bags that invariably explode, not the instant you lift them out of the pail but ten seconds later, over the living room rug, generally when they are filled with giblet gravy, coffee grounds, and diapers laden with baby poo.

Plus, incongruity is funny. We now know that the dangedest men have cheated. Einstein cheated. So did Charles Kuralt, who looked like a lymph node. Bill Cosby, the avatar of fatherhood. Bob Hope. Martin Luther King Jr. Clarence Darrow. Mister Rogers.

GINA: I didn't know Mister Rogers cheated!

GENE: I made that one up. The point is, you were ready to buy it.

GINA: I'm with you so far. Men are bad. Just don't go where I think you are going.

GENE: Where do you think I am going?

GINA: Guess.

GENE: You want me to guess where *you* guess I am going so that you can tell me if I am right about what you presume will be some impending assertion of mine that, *should I make it,* you are likely to consider unacceptable? I think not.

GINA: Fine. You are going to advance the tired old argument that cheating is a genetic imperative. That men just can't help it because they're hardwired to spread their seed indiscriminately so as to maximize genetic mixing, whereas women are programmed for monogamy, so as to ensure a stable environment for child rearing.

GENE:

GINA: Thank you. It's a pretty convenient argument for the fellas, wouldn't you say?

GENE: It's self-evident. It's observable.

GINA: So is a flat earth. Men aren't still squatting on their haunches and spearing wildebeests; there's no reason they should still be serial cheaters. It is the nature of civilization to civilize.

GENE: Do you contend that married women do not cheat?

GINA: Married women cheat in much lower numbers. A lot of married men are apparently doing their cheating with single women. Among people who've had at least one affair, surveys consistently show a three-to-two ratio of married men to married women. But even that's misleadingly low, since men are more likely than women to have several affairs. So there's a multiplier effect for men.

Now, why do you think married men cheat?

GENE: Well, when Hillary Clinton was asked to explain why Bill cheated on her, she theorized that it was because he had grown up under the influence of two domineering women who fought with each other—his mother and grandmother. Hillary was implying that, psychologically, Bill developed the need to seek the affection and approval of more than one woman—eager to please both, and basically losing the ability to say no.

I humbly accept this explanation. Men cheat because they love and respect women and wish to please them. It is essentially altruism.

GINA:

GENE: I'm quoting a noted feminist!

GINA:

GENE: Okay, men cheat because we are overlibidinous, snarfling horndogs. So why do women cheat? I am guessing you will not accept the horndog hypothesis.

GINA: Here's a clue. Would you think that working wives or housewives are more likely to cheat?

GENE: Working wives.

GINA: Why?

GENE: I am applying a basic principle of criminology. Both have motive, but working women also have opportunity. Day to day, they interact with more men.

GINA: Well, you're wrong, Sherlock. Housewives are more likely to cheat. And the reason is that working women already have some concrete, tangible power within their marriage—economic influence. If housewives are to exercise power, they are limited to the only currency they feel they possess. For women, an affair tends to be the result of resentment, an act of complaint, and an assertion of worth.

GENE: For housewives, I would think soap operas enter into it.

GINA: True. You would tend to feel everyone else on earth is cheating but you, so what the hell. My point is that men tend to cheat from positions of power, for reasons linked to self-gratification. Women tend to cheat from positions of powerlessness, for reasons of control.

So even in the tawdry theater of adultery, where no one looks good, a woman's behavior is less selfish. Here's another fact: Even though more men cheat, more marriages break up over the wife's cheating than over the husband's. What would you conclude from that?

GENE: That women are evil.

GINA: You are not doing well here. Personally, I would say that it means women are more forgiving than men and less willing to cavalierly cast away a family. So let's summarize: less selfish, more forgiving, and—here's another one—more remorseful.

One of my favorite scientific studies examined men and women about to break up their marriages. A woman who is planning to leave her husband will spend inordinate amounts of time surveying her girlfriends, and her girlfriends' girlfriends, and the divorced aunts of her daughter's school friends, trying to make a match for her soon-to-be ex. But if a man is planning on leaving his wife at midnight, and it is 11 P.M. and he is at a party where some other guy is hitting on her, he'll punch the guy out. Because to women relationships are about relationships, but to men relationships are about themselves. What's theirs is theirs.

It's why a man loves his car until the minute he sells it, at which point he doesn't give a crap about what happens to it. In fact, he hopes it breaks down two weeks later, because it will confirm how lucky and shrewd he is. He may love his car, but what he loves is *his* car. When a woman sells her house and discovers that the new owners have stripped the wallpaper from the foyer, it's like they've stripped her skin away.

And it's also why men grope.

GENE: Grope?

GINA: We're back to your kissyface bandits. The impulse to cheat and the impulse to grab behinds are not dissimilar. In men, they are based on a desire to own, obtain, win. So if you want to understand why men cheat, observe the actions of the sexual harasser in the workplace. It is primarily an assertion of power and dominion. Copping a feel is not really about sex.

GENE: Copping a feel is not about sex?

GINA: Not really.

GENE: This is one of those absurd feminist pronouncements that men are not allowed even to question. We are expected to nod meekly, so as to demonstrate our sensitivity and our solidarity with the oppressed. Sorry. A woman has roughly the same standing to offer an opinion on these subjects that a jackhammer operator has to discuss recent advances in ophthalmic surgery.

As far as copping a feel not being about sex, I would urge you to consult any sixteen-year-old boy, for whom copping a feel represents a sexual achievement so cataclysmic and overpowering that it can momentarily render him a drooling idiot. This is a reflex arc, far less intense but still present in the adult. Copping a feel is assaultive, disrespectful, and, perhaps most to the point, ludicrously counterproductive as a romantic strategy—but it is definitely about sex. It's even been authenticated. It's second base!

GINA: It is not. It's unwanted. It's not even part of the game.

GENE: Well, it's like *stealing* second base.

GINA: Men love to reduce human relationships to simplistic analogies, usually ones in which women are objectified.

GENE: Such as "Why buy the cow if you get the milk for free"?

GINA: Bingo.

GENE: You don't like that one?

GINA: I won't even address the loathsomeness of the bovinity part. The rest is objectionable because it has been used for generations to restrict young women's freedom of choice. There is no corresponding warning for young men. It is based on a ridiculous misconception about human behavior.

GENE: It may be unfair, but it is true.

GINA: Bull.

GENE: I read surveys, too. A 2002 Rutgers University study shows that men are marrying later because women are more willing to shack up. This isn't good news for older women, the researchers suggest, because as women get older they become less marriageable, whereas as men get older they become more marriageable.

GINA: You have got to be kidding. That was part of the study?

GENE: That's how it was reported.

GINA: This is the classic cultural double standard. The writer Cynthia Heimel makes the point that in the movie *Punchline,* Sally Field played Tom Hanks's love interest, but in their very next movie together—*Forrest Gump*—she played his mom. Society is telling us that at thirty-eight or so, women are no longer beautiful. We cease to be sexual beings and start being maternal.

GENE: Maybe it's true.

GINA: I beg your pardon?

GENE: I am not personally advancing this theory, since I personally intend to maintain a conjugal relationship with my beautiful wife. But, theoretically, what if genetics program us so that a woman is most attractive to men during childbearing years, whereas a man, who is capable of fatherhood into his seventies, will remain attractive to women when older?

GINA: I thought I've made this clear. Life is not a version of *Wild Kingdom.* Women do not fall for older men because they think, "Hey, he can get me pregnant." It's because they think, "Hey, he'll be asleep by seven P.M., which means that I can have a good time with Raimondo, who is out there cleaning the pool that my husband's money paid for."

GENE: Women in their forties do not look with lust at eighteen-year-old pool boys.

GINA: Yes, we do.

GENE: You never admit it.

GINA: We do to each other. It's no different from how middle-aged men lust after eighteen-year-old girls.

GENE: Many men don't. I don't. I have a daughter who is twenty-two. There's a genetic thing that kicks in. Darwin again.

A man will not look with lust at a woman who is less than five years older than his oldest daughter. Any father of an adult girl will confirm this, and he won't be lying. So, as it happens, you are scoping out younger merchandise than I am.

GINA:

GENE: Shame on you.

GINA:

GENE: Whoa. I just won, didn't I?

GINA: Now it's 73–7.

Signs Your Spouse Might Be Cheating on You

(A Weighted Checklist)

- ❏ Your husband starts buying his own underpants. They are colored. [Two points]

- ❏ Your wife goes shopping for five hours, returns home with nothing, and was not mugged for her purchases. [Three points]

- ❏ Your husband brushes his teeth before driving the baby-sitter home. [Four points]

- ❏ For no apparent reason, your wife stops complaining about your little incivilities, such as leaving your underpants on the floor. [Four points]

- ❏ Your husband begins to exhibit knowledge in certain areas that should be unknown territory, such as the difference between a dirndl skirt and an Empire waist. [Four points] VARIATION: He begins to use words or expressions startlingly inappropriate to his age, such as "awesome," or, even worse, "cool" pronounced with two syllables. [Five points]

❏ Your wife is losing weight, is not bragging about it, and does not have a pernicious disease. [Five points]

❏ Your husband starts washing his own underpants. [Six points]

❏ Your wife leaves for work but hurriedly comes back for her diaphragm. [Nine points]

❏ Your husband stops wearing underpants. [Ten points]

❏ You find a man in the closet. He claims to be the "closet repairman." [Twenty-two points]

13

Playing Dumb:
Our Secret Pleasures

GENE: May I ask a nasty question?

GINA: You are asking my permission to be nasty?

GENE: Not really. I'm just being polite.

GINA: You are politely requesting to be impolite?

GENE: I suppose I'm attempting to subvert the rules of engagement. I am hoping to negotiate your acquiescence in advance so that when we are done, readers will be less inclined to dislike me for hitting a girl.

GINA: Fine. Just so we understand each other. Go.

GENE: I have lately been leafing through the best-selling women's magazines in the country—*Cosmo, Vogue,* and so forth. If, as you contend, women are more sophisticated and more civilized and more independent than men, why is it that their reading material of choice is aggressively vapid? Why is it that when women choose to be completely alone with themselves, with no one to impress, so many of them take refuge in these giggly manuals devoted almost exclusively to how to find men, how to seduce men, how to pleasure men, how to keep men, and where to find really cute shoes? These magazines are filled with lists and multiple-choice tests exploring such issues as "Are You Wistful Enough?" and "Is Your Boyfriend Sleeping with Your Aunt?" and "Crying Strategies: 10 That Work."

On a related topic, why is it that women and not men single-handedly support the vast charlatanic industry that spans astrology, crystal therapy, séances, labyrinths, auras, past-life regression, numerology, herbal healing, Zen shiatsu, macrobiotics, therapeutic touching, and tantric yoga, as well as the lion's share of the gigantic publishing scam known as "self-help," which enriches semiliterate emotion racketeers (most of whom are men) who spoon out platitudinous, bromide-laced pablum to a rapt skirt-wearing audience? Why have women made runaway bestsellers out of those "Chicken Soup" books, which should by all rights be modern society's literary emetics?

Why is it, in short, that even intelligent women seem to have this ditz thing going? Why are women so gullible?

GINA: Are you through?

GENE: Also, plug-in air fresheners.

GINA: Women *are* gullible. It is a Darwinian adaptation, because if we were not gullible, the human race would cease to exist.

GENE: Do you embrace and celebrate it?

GINA: No. I admit our gullibility is a shameful weakness. We believe it when a man tells us he loves us, even if we should know he doesn't love us because he has inquired, with elaborate casual interest, if it is true that our sister has a trick pelvis. It is because, at our center, women are attracted by fantasy, because we hunger for an idealized version of the way the world should be if it weren't a place whose rhythms and conventions were dictated by men, with all the accompanying crushing disappointments.

And so, when we are alone in our own heads, with no one to impress, we still play with Barbies. These adult Barbies come in the form of dippy, giggly magazines and New Age pursuits you rightfully find silly. But at least, in our escapism, we still seek meaning and connection. We want to believe it is possible to find inner peace by smelling nice things. We want to believe it is possible to fix our marriage in ten easy steps. We want Mom to tell us, from the grave, how proud she is of us, and how everything is going to be all right. Does that answer your question?

GENE: Actually, yes.

GINA: Are you feeling embarrassed?

GENE: Not that I would admit.

GINA: Now, how's about we discuss men's escapism?

GENE: Aren't you going to ask permission to be nasty?

GINA: No. Now I am entitled. Why don't we discuss what men read when they are alone with themselves, with nobody to impress, if you see what I am saying?

GENE: If you're talking about porn, it's off the point.

GINA: Why?

GENE: Because pornography is not escapism. It is certainly not "reading" material. The verb "read" no more describes what men do with pornography than the verb "dine" describes what a dog does with a stolen rump roast as he runs from the table with angry humans in pursuit.

GINA: Is there a verb you prefer? "Look at"?

GENE: "Look at" implies a casual perusal. There is nothing

casual in the relationship between men and porn. Men "use" pornography. It's a tool. It comes in handy, as it were.

GINA: Fine. Would you care to explain or defend on purely logical grounds the fact that men, and men alone, finance a multibillion-dollar industry whose entire purpose is to produce and distribute visual images of objects so commonplace that they exist at all times on the bodies of fully half the people on the planet? Or that this hunger has virtually hijacked the Internet, filling our in-baskets with invitations to watch teenagers do it with a horse? Do you embrace and celebrate this?

GENE: No.

GINA: Do you deny that it is an entirely male obsession?

GENE: I wish I could. I cannot.

Women are, at their heart, exhibitionists. Men are, at their heart, voyeurs. And pornography, at its own skanky heart, is the ultimate in voyeurism. Porn is peeking, and men are addicted to peeking.

The best example of this is evident on any vehicle of public transportation. If a pretty woman is seated across from a man and she is wearing shorts and her legs are crossed, the man will take notice, but with casual interest. However, if she is wearing a *skirt* and crossing her legs—showing less thigh than would be shown in the shorts—the guy is enslaved. He secretly monitors her every movement, in case by some subtle shifting of position she might display a few more square inches of leg, though *still* less than she would in shorts. This is because the shorts are a straightforward invitation to look, but the skirt is forbidden. With the skirt, he is peeking. He may as well be sitting there leafing through *Hustler.*

Women simply lack this impulse. I have a friend—a genteel, urbane professional woman with a suburban nuclear family—who confessed to me one day that she enjoys Internet porn. I was stunned. Frankly, I was delighted. It turns out, however, that she was talking about downloading ribald passages from trashy French novels and reading them *in French* as both entertainment and language instruction.

GINA: Right. Self-help. To most women, Anaïs Nin qualifies as pornography, whereas men require something a great deal more indelicate.

So let's examine the souls of organisms who are routinely turned on, like toggle switches, not by beautiful erotic writing, the caress of a loved one, or paintings and sculpture that artistically celebrate the sensuality of the human form, but by close-up pictures of labia. Let us try to imagine the complexity of these organisms—the contours of their internal landscape, the texture of the philosophies by which they live.

Here's an instructive true story. Some time ago, I hired a stonemason to repair a chimney. He was a nice guy, a large, laconic man with subtle skills who lived by his hands and worked only when he needed to, maintaining a simple, Spartan lifestyle. He was refreshingly honest and without pretension. He told me, for example, that he no longer worked during the winter because he had gotten too fat to fit into his orange winter jumpsuit. I encouraged conversation. I actually saw it as an opportunity to plumb the mind of a typical man, maybe soften some of my prejudices.

One day he came to me, genuinely excited, wishing to discuss a scientific matter. He had read somewhere that in the foreseeable future it might be possible to transplant one person's brain into someone else's body. He seemed intrigued by the philosophical ramifications of this. I could well imagine: The ethical and moral questions alone could fill a medical journal, not to mention issues about the very nature of identity. "Exactly, exactly," he said. I could see he was reaching within himself, excited to share his insights.

"Here's the thing," he said finally, quite earnest. "I could be happy for the rest of my life if they transplanted my brain into the body of a seventeen-year-old girl. I'd never leave the house. I'd spend all day feeling myself up."

GENE: Wow.

GINA: Appalled?

GENE: Impressed. He's my hero. A philosopher-king.

GINA: What we have here is evidence that when you reach down into a man, you come up empty.

GENE: You do not. There's plenty of stuff down there. You just don't want to go poking around in it too much.

GINA: I think we've come quite a way in this conversation, don't you? We began by dismantling the thesis that women are ditzes, and ended by establishing fairly convincingly that men are slime. I think my work here is done. Have you anything to say for yourself or your sex at this time, any logical, coherent response that seriously answers any of my assertions or suggests in any way that I am in error? I urge you to draw from whatever scientific or literary arsenal you have at your disposal, including the writings of Plutarch. Summon the muses. Consult your friends and colleagues. Marshal your weaponry and hit me with the most intellectually cogent argument you've got.

GENE: *Gina* is an anagram for "I nag."

Signs Your Wife or Girlfriend Might Be Addicted to Idiot Women's Magazines

❏ She asks you to "grade your orgasms."

❏ She has a collection of Hummel figurines in the shape of the cast of *Friends* or a set of Winnie-the-Pooh characters made of semiprecious stone. She pays for these things on an easy monthly plan.

❏ She attempts to convince you that the back of your neck is the most sensitive erogenous zone.

❏ During lovemaking, she asks you to move your "loins."

❏ She seems to believe she has a "destiny," and that rearranging her throw pillows will change it.

Signs Your Husband or Boyfriend Might Be Addicted to Porn

❏ In the throes of passion, he yells out "July!"

❏ He wants you to wear spike heels, and only spike heels, in bed. He seems to think this is normal.

❏ He asks you if you were ever a "teen nymph slut."

❏ When he goes down on you, he calls this "a close-up."

❏ At night, he is always on the computer. Literally ON the computer.

14

The Joy of Sexism
(Part I—Jokes That Offend
Women)

GENE: Why do women have vaginas?

GINA: You *don't know* why women have vaginas?

GENE: It's a joke.

GINA: Oh. I know this joke.

GENE: Right, but some of the readers might not. Why do women have vaginas?

GINA: I'm not participating. It's a foul joke.

GENE: I don't think it is. It's a pretty good joke, and from it we can learn something about how men and women regard humor. Just play along, okay?

GINA: Women have been "just playing along" for years, and it hasn't gotten us very far.

GENE: It's just a joke!

GINA: It's a revolting joke. It's a perfect example of the way men use so-called humor to objectify and marginalize women,

and then criticize women as humorless prunes for not seeing the nonexistent humor in it.

GENE: Well, then you can use this nonjoke to convince everyone what an insensitive lout I am, and all men by extension. Why do women have vaginas?

GINA: *I DON'T KNOW, GENE. WHY DO WOMEN HAVE VAGINAS?*

GENE: So men will talk to them.

GINA: As I said, disgusting.

GENE: Explain why. Explain why women hear this joke and decide it is an appalling attack upon women.

GINA: It is self-evident.

GENE: Please. For all us nitwits.

GINA: Because it advances the contention that the only value women have is as sperm receptacles. Because it suggests that any relationship at all between a man and a woman, from casual conversation to cohabitation, occurs only because men feel they have to flatter us into thinking they find us interesting—whereas, in fact, they are merely attempting to maneuver us into bed, confident that we are so stupid that we will never understand their true motivations.

GENE: So you think this joke would be funny only to troglodytes who share this view of women—snouted, oinking ungulates such as myself?

GINA: Yes.

GENE: Does your highly evolved college professor husband share that view of women?

GINA: He does not.

GENE: Are you sure?

GINA: Yes.

GENE: Go tell him the joke and ask him if it is funny. I'll wait right here.

GINA: Hang on.

GENE: Tum te tum . . .

GINA: He says yes.

GENE: Now, how do you suppose that could be? Either you are tragically mistaken about the man you have chosen for your life partner, or just possibly there is a slightly different engine of humor at work here from the one you see.

I believe the reason this joke is funny is that it is wonderfully concise. It condenses the whole axiom about how a woman will have sex with a man as a means to obtain, she hopes, personal intimacy and companionship, while a man will provide personal intimacy and companionship as a means to obtain, he hopes, sex. This is nothing more nor less than a translation into modern vernacular of the quote I attributed to Anonymous in Chapter 11, to which you had no objection.

In short, I believe this is not a joke at the expense of women, but one at the expense of both men and women, because of the silly dance we do. If anything, it is harder on the men, since the women's needs and desires are more about connection and redemption and less about self-gratification.

GINA: Very, very fancy.

GENE: Thank you.

GINA: I do not buy it for a minute.

GENE: I think you know I am right.

GINA: Even if you are right, you chose the joke to illustrate your point. There is a whole trove of disgusting humor that belittles women.

GENE: Much of it is similarly misinterpreted. People should not be afraid of humor. People should not be poised to take offense.

GINA: Why don't you tell the one you told me about the three tampons walking down the street?

GENE:

GINA: Go ahead. The whole class is waiting

GENE:

GINA: I'll be delighted to be your straight woman. And then you can explain how respectful to women this joke is. Or are you . . . afraid?

GENE: Three tampons are walking down the street. Which one will talk to you?

GINA: I don't know, Gene. Which one?

GENE:

GINA: I can't hear you.

GENE: I need to explain something first. To the reader.

GINA: You have no idea how much I am enjoying this.

GENE: Yes, I do. Reader, I need to explain that there's going to be a word in the punch line that many reasonable people might find objectionable.

GINA: No problem. Those who are easily offended will please proceed directly to Chapter 18, which is perfectly wholesome. In fact, for the purpose of scientific inquiry, I will absolve you of blame for what you are about to say and encourage women readers to do the same. Please tell us which one of the tampons will talk to you.

GENE: None of them. They are all stuck up cunts.

GINA: Thank you. Now, was that funny?

GENE: Yes. I'm afraid it was.

GINA: It was not.

GENE: Ask your husband.

GINA: Hang on.

GENE: Tum te tum . . .

GINA: He says it is "very funny." This is getting annoying. Are you going to argue that this is not at the expense of women?

GENE: I am. First, obviously, the joke is a pretty clever play on words. But it's funny on a second level altogether, the level that gives it power. On that level, it's delivered at the expense not of women but of a certain kind of man. This guy is a feeb, a man who cannot score with women because he has no presence or prospects or social skills, and who is forever blaming his strike-outs on the fact that women who ignore him are "stuck up."

The expression "she's just a stuck-up cunt" is the anthem of the male loser. All men know this kind of guy and have contempt for him. All men believe they are not this kind of guy, though many are. This is precisely the type of man who uses the *c*-word in a hostile fashion. We recognize him in this joke—the joke teller is, in effect, *becoming* him and inviting ridicule.

GINA: One, I don't believe that, and two, the word itself is demeaning. When a woman is called a "cunt," it is invariably hostile. It is defining a woman as nothing but her sexual organs. Men are happy to be defined by their sexual organs—they have no problem thinking of themselves as dicks in hats. Women, however, do not like this.

GENE: We are in interesting territory here, with sexual organs and language. In a spasm of misguided propriety some years ago, a male editor at *The Washington Post* instructed that, for reasons of delicacy, the word *vagina* could not appear in a story about the female condom. He felt *vagina* was a bad word, a vulgar word, unfit for publication in a family newspaper. The writer, who happened to be a woman, quite rationally argued that it was difficult if not impossible to describe how this product is used—it is inserted into the vagina prior to intercourse—without mentioning, y'know, the aperture into which it is inserted.

The editor grumbled, grabbed the story, and rewrote it himself. So the published version reports that the female condom is positioned in such a way that it "lines the inside of a woman." In a good-faith but boneheaded effort to show sensitivity, this editor created a sentence—now forever archived in *The Washington Post*—in which "woman" is synonymous with "vagina."

GINA: That's excellently stupid. But what's your point?

GENE: My point is that there are no "bad words," and that all words must be judged in the context in which they are used. In the tampon joke, I contend the *c*-word is used with no disrespect toward women. The disrespect is toward the man who would utter it. Still, I acknowledge that to virtually all women, this word is instantly repugnant.

I would not tell this joke to a woman who was not my significant other, or with whom I was not writing a book about humor, or in any public context other than a serious discussion of the meaning of the joke. But whether or not you find the word offensive, I contend that the *engine* of the joke itself is not hostile to women. In fact, it is exactly the opposite.

GINA: Even a dirty standup comic would not tell that joke.

GENE: I agree. But it is not because of any inherent problem with the joke. It is because he knows that women—correctly or incorrectly—will find this joke offensive. A stand-up comic is not a theoretician or an epistemologist. He is not onstage to defend his craft or analyze his humor. He is a businessman who depends on the goodwill of his audience. And stand-up comics have a certain rule—they ignore women's sensibilities at their own risk.

Here is why: If you are making the men laugh but making the women uncomfortable, the men will eventually stop laughing. And the room will become excruciatingly quiet. This is because it may well be a night out at the comedy club, but it is still a date— with all the attendant hopes and stratagems.

GINA: Interesting. We are back to sexual stratagems. Why do women have vaginas?

GENE: Well, yes. It all comes down to that. I am not arguing there are no stratagems. I am arguing that the existence of stratagems does not imply contempt. Stratagems are part of the game. It is possible for a man to play football without losing respect for his opponent.

GINA: Is it possible for a man to make a point without resorting to some lame sports metaphor?

GENE: It's hard. To make a point, you've got to touch the ball. Wait, come to think of it, you can get two points if the punter misses the snap and the ball rolls through the end zone for a safety without your ever touching it. So yes, I would say it is possible. But rare.

15

The Joy of Sexism (Part II—Jokes That Castrate Men)

GINA: I just had a messy divorce.

GENE: You got divorced?

GINA: This is a joke.

GENE: I thought women didn't tell jokes.

GINA: Mostly, women tell stories. But sometimes we tell jokes, and they're funny, and men could learn a little something from them. I just had a messy divorce.

GENE: You got divorced?

GINA:

GENE: Okay, okay. *Why was your divorce messy, Gina?*

GINA: Because there was a child involved: my husband.

GENE: Ah.

GINA: You don't find that funny?

GENE: Well, it's not pants-wettingly funny, like the three tampons joke.

GINA: It always gets a big laugh when I use it in speeches to large rooms filled with professional women.

GENE: Tell another one. This may prove productive.

GINA: Why do Kennedy men cry when making love?

GENE: Why?

GINA: Mace.

GENE: I like it. Another.

GINA: What am I, your clown? Do I *amuse* you?

GENE: We're actually making headway in our good-faith efforts to understand the gender divide in humor. Humor me. As it were.

GINA: A woman walks into a hardware store and asks for a hinge. The clerk says, "Want a screw for that?" And she says, "No, but I'll blow you for a toaster."

GENE: Excellent. Another joke women like, please.

GINA: A woman is in the dentist's chair, and as the dentist bends over with the drill, she slowly, seductively, unzips his fly and maneuvers her hand inside. He is startled but makes no move to stop her. Purring, she gently caresses his testicles. As he starts to work, a new smile on his face, she says, "Now, we're not going to hurt each other, are we, Doctor?"

GENE: One more, and our work here is done.

GINA: A man has two employees, Debra and Jack. Both are good workers, but budget restraints are forcing him to let one of them go. He decides he is going to explain the situation to both, on the chance that one might be thinking of leaving anyway. Debra gets to work first, so he calls her in and says, "I'm afraid I'm either going to have to lay you or Jack off." She says, "Just jack off, okay? I have a headache."

GENE: Okay. They're all funny. But as a student of humor,

---

would you not agree that there is one dominant theme that links them all?

GINA: What's that?

GENE: Hint: It is a *dominant* theme.

GINA: If you mean they place women in a position of power, I would agree. In each case, the woman ultimately controls the action.

GENE: A man less charitable than I might suggest that there is a political ethic at work in women's humor, a Stalinist party line: women on top. I would not personally make such an observation. But how would you respond to some darn sexist clown who did?

GINA: It is no party line. No one is ordering women to find this funny. We find it funny because it is funny, and it is funny because of its incongruity. We know that in our culture, women *aren't* on top. So these jokes are saying that if you stand the world on its head, this is what it looks like. It is the humor of inversion.

GENE: I am not questioning why women find these jokes funny. I find them funny, too. I am questioning why women find *only* these types of jokes funny. Ninety-five percent of all women's humor involves relationships.

GINA: And imbalances of power.

GENE: In relationships.

GINA: Yes.

GENE: Plus, there seems to be, as a necessary theme, a strong or subtle hostility to men.

GINA: It is not hostility. It is not even attitude. It is reporting how things are. It is journalism. These jokes are practically documentaries.

GENE: In any case, the range isn't very wide. Men's humor is less limited. Men tell jokes about golf. Do women?

GINA: No.

GENE: Priest, rabbi?

GINA: No.

GENE: Poo?

GINA: No.

GENE: Ethnic disparagement?

GINA: No.

GENE: The comedy of tragedy?

GINA: No.

GENE: Quite limited, if you ask me.

GINA: Self-limited, by discernment and taste. What you call eclecticism I would call promiscuity. Do you consider yourself an arbiter of what is funny and what is not?

GENE: Well, yes.

GINA: Of course you do. Men do. With humor, women will express preferences, but men will hand down verdicts. They consider their humor paradigmatic pronouncements. It is symptomatic of a larger cultural conditioning.

Women will go into an overheated room and say, "Is it hot, or is it me?" Other women will be sweating like stevedores, and they will all be seeking each other out for opinions on the heat, making sure everyone is included in the decision over the thermostat setting. Ballots will be photocopied and passed around, so as not to disenfranchise those too timid to speak up. A man walks into a room and feels too hot, he'll put a fist through a window if he can't get it open.

GENE: I think you are attempting to make a point.

GINA: It's the same thing with humor. Male humor is a guy putting a fist through a window. A solitary, unsubtle act of an angry guy. Women's humor tends to be the result of consensus and collaboration. Male humor is two-dimensional. And the reason it is two-dimensional is that it lacks the healthful benefit of depth and texture that can be developed only through cooperative effort.

Watch a group of men standing around telling jokes, and what you are looking at is a competition: "Okay, I got one for you. . . ." They are trying to best each other. When women tell jokes or funny stories, it becomes a quilting bee.

GENE: A quilting bee?

GINA: I wish I hadn't said that. But it's true. Everyone is adding her story to this bigger picture. As the bigger picture takes shape, it is often about power imbalances.

GENE: The Stalinist party line.

GINA: The socialist collective. The eternal cry of the oppressed and marginalized. It's a covert method of telling your story. Slaves invented the blues to cope with their privation. Russian humor of the 1950s was all about breadlines, bureaucratic incompetence, and the overbearing arrogance of the party. Women tell jokes about their lack of power.

GENE: So let's get this straight. If you and I are both right, men tell jokes that seem to marginalize women but really are laughing at themselves and what pigs they can be. And women tell jokes that seem to be about strong women but really are laughing at how oppressed they are by men, who are pigs. So, basically, men take it coming and going.

GINA: I would say, yes, "coming" and "going" seem to embody most of men's eclectic range of humor, yes.

GENE: Nice.

GINA: Thank you.

GENE: Can we end this fight with a joke that both men and

women can embrace? What would that involve? I ask you because this entails a complicated enforced political calculus.

GINA: Let's see. Men would have to be pigs, but firmly in control. The joke would have to establish as an immutable fact that the social order oppresses women, and yet do so in a fashion that underscores the injustice of it and women's powerlessness in its face. It can contain playful vulgarity, but no shockingly offensive or hostile terminology. It should be delivered with a hint of apology, a suggestion that the teller feels guilt, though he may also feel permission to gloat. The woman can be victimized but not humiliated.

GENE: Does the joke teller have to dress a certain way, Mistress Gina?

GINA: You asked, I answered.

GENE: Joe is interviewing three women for an important job requiring both resourcefulness and unimpeachable moral character. He decides to give them an ethics test. He asks each one the same question: If you found that an extra thousand dollars had been accidentally added to one of your paychecks, what would you do? The first applicant said she would return it immediately. The second said she would put it in the bank but not touch it for a year so that she could return it, with interest, if the error was caught. The third said that she presumed he wanted honesty, and her honest answer was that she would spend it immediately on a luxury and refuse to give it back if asked, both because she felt that was her legal right and because suffering that loss might well impel the company to improve its accounting practices.

The question is, which woman did he hire?

GINA: I don't know. Which?

GENE: The one with the great ass.

GINA: I like it.

GENE: Me too.

GINA: That's kind of exciting.

GENE: Let's have sex.

GINA: Not that exciting.

16

A Short Commercial Break

GENE: I am looking at an advertisement in *Index,* an international arts magazine. The ad is for Gucci, a company that to my knowledge is famous mostly for its handbags, yet there isn't a handbag in sight. What is in sight is a woman wearing a kimono. You see her only from the neck down, but you know she is a woman because the kimono is sufficiently open in the front to reveal that she has a bosom, and because her legs look very much like women's legs, and because she has hooked a thumb into her underpants and is pulling them down far enough for you to realize that: (1) this can *only* be a woman, and (2) her pubic hair has been shaved and sculpted into the *G* of the Gucci logo.

When this ad debuted in England not long ago, it was a prude awakening. Complaints were filed. Authorities were alerted. Somehow, peace was maintained.

When I first saw this ad, my first act was to alert Gina, because I realized that here was a chance to register my solidarity with women worldwide and express my outrage at the advertising industry's blatant and insupportable objectification of the female sex.

GINA:

GENE: What?

GINA: Tell them what your first act really was, even before you called me.

GENE: I showed it to my son.

GINA: And what did your son do with it?

GENE: He took it with him back to college.

GINA: Like the proverbial dog scurrying away with the proverbial stolen rump roast?

GENE: Yes.

GINA: Good. Now tell us all what you *really* thought when you saw the ad.

GENE: Gonna get me some Gucci. Gonna accessorize like there's no tomorrow. Gonna buy me some of them Gucci pocketbooks and belts and totes and fragrances and Gucci "timepieces," which are exactly like "watches," only much more expensive. Gonna get me one of them $5,000 Gucci western saddles. Gonna buy me a horse and name him Goochie.

GINA: Thank you.

GENE: You do not approve of this ad?

GINA: I do not. And perhaps the best argument for *why* I do not approve of it was eloquently made by Gucci's own CEO, Tom Ford. He made it while defending the ad, which he entertainingly calls "The G Spot," in an interview with *The Sunday Times* of London. The ad, he said, is a fabulously successful way to get the brand name out there. It is, as he put it, "the ultimate in branding."

He's right. It might as well have said "The Lazy Q Ranch." The model was a head of cattle, and Gucci was declaring ownership. Her face was of such little consequence that it was cropped out, which is the art director's version of a paper bag. This was crotch as billboard. Her identity was irrelevant. It's not even like it's her initial.

GENE: So if her name was, say, Gina, it would be okay?

GINA: Don't even go there.

GENE: Yes'm.

GINA: Are you going to *defend* this ad?

GENE: I am. I think this ad is playfully life-affirming. It celebrates our lust to survive. Sexual desire does not degrade our species, it ennobles it. Our hunger to survive is what created our hunger for each other, which is what created love, which has informed song and poetry and literature throughout the millennia. Love and lust are the most powerful literary inspirations we have, other than, perhaps, death. On this intense battleground, our sex drive wars with our mortality—and, as the march of civilization attests, triumphs over it. Gucci is boldly drawing from that energy and owes no apology to anyone.

GINA:

GENE: What?

GINA: You're full of shit.

GENE: Gonna get me some Gucci.

GINA: The sad fact is that men have been conditioned to accept in advertising a sort of casual, even ritual sexism that they would condemn in the workplace or classroom.

GENE: It's because ads perform in a different theater. Ads are not real. They require a suspension of disbelief. Every package of toilet paper features a picture of a baby, even though babies are the only people who never use the product. We understand ads are metaphorical.

But more important, these ads operate through humor, and the humor is good-natured. The Gucci ad is good-natured, and so is that famous male-fantasy TV ad where two elegantly dressed women begin arguing about whether Miller Lite's most valuable attribute is that it is less filling or that it tastes great—and they wind up ripping each other's clothes off and wrestling in the mud. It's funny, and it's playfully funny. It is not sexist because the message is a joke, and the joke is that men are dorks.

GINA: The message is: "Men are dorks, now show me your tits." That is not playful sexism, that is aggressive sexism, and it is disingenuously crafted the way it is so that the *ultimate* message is the same obnoxious one it has always been: "What's the matter, honey, don't you have a sense of humor?"

Have you ever been to a car show? Car manufacturers invariably put their new models out on the floor with human models, curvy ones in sequined dresses that hug their behinds. I have been to these shows, and I have talked to these women afterward. And do you know what they say? They all report that during the show, men will sidle up to the display, check out the cars, and then—all of them, construction workers, accountants, visiting Sri Lankan agronomists—say the same thing to the women. They all say, thinking it rib-ticklingly funny and original: "Do you come with the car?"

Modern advertising is presenting women as accessories. Like a Gucci bag.

GENE: Honestly, you can't look at this Gucci ad and see anything of value?

GINA: There are two small elements that are positive. But they are of negligible importance.

GENE: Go.

GINA: Well, do you like displays of pubic hair?

GENE: Under certain circumstances.

GINA: That the hair in question belongs to an attractive woman?

GENE: Those would be the circumstances.

GINA: This is the first small area in which this ad illustrates progress. The very fact that you have the opportunity to publicly observe and admire female pubic hair is a surprisingly modern phenomenon. For much of Western history, it was impermissible even to publicly acknowledge the presence of it.

GENE: Why?

GINA: Because men preferred not to. It made them uncomfortable, because they wanted their women tidy, and pubic hair was untidy. And so men crafted the image of women that they preferred, simply because they had the power to do so. The reality was icky to them, so they changed it. They created their idealized female form, as celebrated in paintings and sculpture. In these representations, women are shown with their crotches obscured by leaf or hand or fold of cloth, or, most commonly, they are simply shown hairless as a baby, with legs positioned so labia are hidden. Classic nude statuary of men often included pubic hair—Michelangelo's *David,* for example—but female statuary did not.

And so unless one had the opportunity to observe women intimately in the flesh, a man could actually remain ignorant of pubic hair. The British art critic John Ruskin wedded the lovely Euphermia Gray on April 10, 1854. Their marriage lasted only days. It was never consummated. Ruskin had it annulled because he was horrified to behold upon his bride a thatch of hair, rough and wild, similar to a man's. He thought her a monster.

Though thirty-five, Ruskin evidently had had no sexual experience beforehand—or if he had, it was of the furtive, groping-in-the-dark nature common to his time. Of course, he *had* seen and inspected thousands of nudes on museum walls and atop sconces and in grottoes. Alas, they had offered him no useful guidance.

So, yes. Hooray. The Gucci ad acknowledges our pubes.

GENE: And its second redeeming characteristic?

GINA: I'm not sure I really want to get into the second one. You will misinterpret it, either through ignorance or to further an intellectually dishonest argument.

GENE: You've gone too far now.

GINA: Well, the second point is pretty obvious. The guy.

GENE: What guy?

GINA: The guy in the ad.

GENE: There was a guy?

GINA: I can see how you didn't notice. He only takes up half the page. He is kneeling in front of the woman, looking wistful. He is a supplicant. His eyes appear riveted upon the main source of contention in this ad. Look again.

GENE: You're right. In fact, one could conclude from his position that he is about to render her a certain personal service.

GINA: I agree that would be a reasonable conclusion.

GENE: This would be the particular personal service that many feminists contend modern men are too unwilling to provide, even though they would expect their women to administer the analogous service at any and all times.

GINA: That is correct.

GENE: So the ad, in effect, makes the articulate case for gender equality!

GINA: I knew you would say that.

GENE: It puts the woman in the power position.

GINA: It does not. This is so transparent. Gucci uncovered her crotch, so now they have to cover their own butt. It's manipulative. The fact is, neither of these people is in a power position. They are both in a submissive position to Gucci.

GENE: When you use it that way, "Gucci" almost sounds like a verb.

GINA: It does, now that you mention it. But my point is that the company is just jerking the reader around.

GENE: Actually, in a sense—

GINA: Don't even go there.

GENE: Yes'm.

GINA: The fact is, the Gucci ad is sexist, and the women mud-wrestling over beer is sexist. You will never see an ad in which men are presented in as degrading a fashion, and you know it.

GENE: Yes'm.

GINA: That's it? You concede?

GENE: I don't know why, but I am feeling curiously submissive.

GINA: Then you can help me write an ad that the world will never see, but should.

GENE: Yes'm.

Gene and Gina's Ad We'd Like to See

Fade in . . .

Living room of a suburban home. At mid-distance, we see the back of the head of KATHARINE, thirty-five, in a recliner, watching Oprah on TV. Enter husband IRV, thirty-eight, balding, a little shlumpy, carrying a laundry basket with folded clothing. He stops, as though he has just realized something.

>   IRV
> Hey, honey?

>   KATHARINE
> *(not turning from screen)*
> Yeah?

>   IRV
> Aren't you almost out of tampons?

>   KATHARINE
> *(same)*
> Yeah.

>   IRV
> I'm going to the grocery, I'll pick some
> up for you. I hope you've stopped using
> the ones with the irritating applicator.

KATHARINE
(*switching stations*)
Yeah. I'm using Tampax now.

IRV
The biodegradable kind?

KATHARINE
Yeah.

IRV
You'll need me to get you both regular
and superabsorbent for those heavy-flow
days, right?

KATHARINE
(*still not turning*)
Yeah.

IRV
(*rummages in pocket, withdraws something,
smiles*)
I even kept a coupon!

Doorbell rings. IRV answers it. It is their neighbor
STEVE, twenty-five, a handsome, buff weight lifter type.

STEVE
Hey, Irv.
(*noticing coupon*)

Whoa. I see Katharine uses tampons.
Jessica will only use a pad.

IRV
Jessica's living in the dark ages, Steve.
Katharine and I have been really happy
since we switched to Tampax.

STEVE
I am going to take my shirt off now for
no reason.
(He does. Nice pecs.)

IRV
I see you have a tattoo of an eagle. I had
some body work done, too.

IRV drops his pants, hooks his thumb over his briefs,
and pulls them down to reveal that his pubic hair is
sculpted into the letter *T* of the Tampax logo.

STEVE
Man, I gotta get one of those.

KATHARINE
(still not turning around)
Haven't you left yet?
Fade to logo and slogan: "Tampax. Because He Wants
You to Be Happy."

17

Sports, Penises, and Other Extremities

GENE: On this same weekend that my hometown University of Maryland men's basketball team won the national championship, Gina's hometown University of Connecticut women's basketball team won the national championship. This provides a terrific opportunity to discuss men and women in sports in a respectful and enlightened fashion.

GINA: A man can no more discuss women and sports in a respectful and enlightened fashion than a vulture can eat a dead buffalo with gentility and grace.

GENE: Nonsense. Men have come a long way since they considered women's sports a curiosity, like donkey basketball. Men now acknowledge its legitimacy.

GINA: Only kicking and screaming. The Supreme Court forced you to.

GENE: True. Title IX makes sure that the same amount of money is spent in colleges on women's athletics as on men's. But we can all see the fairness in that. There is no reason that college football should be more heavily funded than synchronized nagging, or whatever it is you gals are into these days.

GINA:

GENE: Kidding, kidding. Nothing could better demonstrate the validity of women's sports than the strength of your college's extraordinary women's basketball program. Our hats are off to it, and to women athletes the world over.

GINA:

GENE: The plucky little dears.

GINA: Are you through?

GENE: I just think it's appropriate to point out that if the national men's champion University of Maryland Terrapins played the national women's champion University of Connecticut Gossiping Fawns, or whatever they're called, the score would be as lopsided as a Dodge Caravan with severe right-side sidewall damage caused by improper parallel parking. It would be an annihilation.

GINA: A rhinoceros can kill a human. It doesn't mean the human is a less legitimate life form.

GENE: Women's sports are just like men's sports, except they are practiced by individuals who are biologically weaker and slower. At the peak levels of performance, there is no comparison. When she was the number-one tennis player in the world, Chris Evert could not defeat her husband or her brother, each a pro of marginal skill. Just as I would not expect women to watch men compete at singing coloratura arias, I wouldn't expect a large male audience to watch what is, essentially, a lesser event.

Men will watch women in the Olympics, but there's a measure

of patriotic rooting there. Plus, a significant number of women in tutus skating backward. But with pro or college sports, men want to see the best. We take it very, very seriously.

GINA: You certainly do. It is among men's least appealing traits.

My husband once informed me with great pride that I was born during one of the very best years for American cars. How do you think this made me feel?

GENE: Hot and sleek?

GINA: More or less. Some women would react poorly to such a thing, but I was fine with it. Do you know why? Because Michael, bless his nearly perfect soul, did *not* tell me that I was born during the year Willie Mays hit seventy-six ground-rule triples, or whatever. Michael does not possess the idiot sports gene. He does possess the idiot *car* gene, but I accept it with gratitude.

There are times, such as when he is entertaining me with details of the performance of a particular automobile, when I must crank up the calliope in my head. It plays a pleasant pipe-organ tune that drowns out disagreeable things. The calliope is a very effective marital aid.

GENE: No sports at all? Aren't you worried he isn't, y'know, all guy?

GINA: My guy is all guy. He has other idiot guy genes, too. I have actually accompanied him on the "duck tour" of Seattle.

GENE: Wow.

GINA: Love enters into this.

GENE: I understand.

GINA: The lack of a sports gene is an erotic quality in a man.

GENE: To me, it's suspicious. In the absence of a sports gene, I demand additional proof of masculinity. My friend David Montgomery, who sits next to me at work, worried me for two years. No sports enthusiasm whatsoever. Then, just a few weeks ago, all my doubts evaporated when David came to work and reported the events of the previous day.

His job had been to get his four-year-old daughter up and out to day care. David is a conscientious father, and he did well. He not only woke Lily and fed her and dressed her, but he dropped her off right on time. Sometime afterward, as she was having lunch, Lily looked down and burst into tears. The teacher ran over and asked what was wrong.

"Daddy brought me to school in my pajamas!"

GINA: All guy.

GENE: Total stud.

GINA: See, one doesn't need sports.

GENE: Even if it is possible to be male without sports, sports are central to the male experience.

GINA: I am not arguing that. They *are* central. It is why you guys are so pathetic. Explain to me, for example, why men insanely wrap their egos up with the performance of a particular sports team. Why do you watch a game and say, "We won"? If you go to see a Broadway musical, you don't come back and say, "Hey, I really sang well last night."

GENE: It's because men are not really rooting for the team. This is a common misconception. We are rooting for our own judgment in aligning with a team, and for our loyalty in sticking with them. We are rooting for ourselves. I would not expect a woman to understand this subtlety any more than I would expect a woman to understand the time-honored male ritual of postvictory vandalism and looting.

GINA: Women do not vandalize or loot. A woman's version of postgame anarchy would be to go shopping impolitely. We would descend on the department stores' cosmetics counters, demand all the samples at once, and apply them indiscriminately.

Women like women's sports, but to them it is entertainment. But women *love* shopping. Shopping is to women what sports are to men. In fact, to women, shopping *is* a sport. I just got back from Nashville with a pair of earrings made from bullets. I spent five dollars for them. I would have easily paid fifty dollars. When I show them to my friends, they'll high-five me. Score! I won!

That's as close as women get to the sort of excess you show with sports.

GENE: Sports does not even come close to the extremes of male excess.

GINA: I'm not talking about war.

GENE: Neither am I. I am talking about the domestic equivalent.

Some time ago, I got an e-mail at work with the subject line GREAT MALE ACHIEVEMENT!!! I almost erased it unread because, in my experience, most unsolicited e-mails with subjects like GREAT MALE ACHIEVEMENT!!! wind up involving opportunities for personal growth, if you get my drift. But this was legit. It included a photograph of the achievement.

GINA: What achievement?

BERNIE: My achievement.

GINA: Who are you?

GENE: He's the guy who sent the e-mail. Bernie Crane, this is Gina.

BERNIE: Hi.

GINA: Hi. Will someone tell me what's going on here?

GENE: Tell her, Bernie. Tell her about your achievement.

BERNIE: I parallel-parked my car in a space so tight that when I was done, the bumpers of my car were touching the bumpers of cars in front and behind. People who were watching applauded.

GINA: Oh, for God's sake.

GENE: Bernie, how long did it take you?

GINA: *Who cares?*

BERNIE: About six or seven minutes. There was a little bit of nudging forward and rolling back involved. Though not, I hesitate to add, of sufficient violence to constitute an actionable assault upon the property of others.

GENE: Bernie is a lawyer. Tell me, Bernie, did you have a sense you were doing something special? As it was happening?

BERNIE: Not initially, but after the fifth or sixth back-and-forth, there was a kind of electricity, like I was on the verge of greatness. There was a guy in a little sports car who was waiting smugly for the spot. I was in a minivan. After a while, he just gave up and left. That was a great moment.

GINA: This is unbelievably moronic.

BERNIE: That's exactly what my sister said. She called me a "nut case."

GINA: She was too kind.

GENE: Bernie the Attorney gets first runner-up in the category of Distinguished Ultra-Male Behavior.

GINA: First runner-up?

BERNIE: Only first runner-up?

GENE: I have the winner standing by. His name is Seth Brown. Say howdy, Seth.

SETH: Howdy.

GINA: Can I leave now?

GENE: You have to hear Seth's story. Seth is twenty-four. He's a freelance writer in Williamstown, Massachusetts. His roommate Tom is an artist. The two guys don't see much of their third roommate, Mandy, so they pretty much are in charge of their own upkeep, which suits them just fine, thank you. It's not like guys can't fend for themselves.

GINA: This is going to be ugly.

GENE: Seth has taken over the cooking chores, and for months he and Tom ate splendidly, without female accompaniment or advice. Tell Gina what you guys ate.

SETH: Potatoes. Fried, sometimes baked. Salt, vinegar. We've got a dish called Smoky Cowboy Rice and Beans. And burritos. I fry burritos with beans and rice and whatever else is on hand. Beef. Eggs. You know.

GENE: Fruits and veggies?

SETH: No.

GENE: Why not?

SETH: Too much hassle.

GENE: Good reason! So, Seth, things were going great until one day something happened. Can you tell the readers what happened?

SETH:

GENE: Don't be bashful.

SETH: We got scurvy.

GENE: Indeed. Swollen gums, loose teeth, mouth sores?

SETH: Yeah.

GENE: A disease not seen in civilized countries since it afflicted filthy eighteenth-century European sailors! Seth wins first prize in the category of Distinguished Ultra-Male Behavior!

SETH: Wow. Thanks.

GENE: Tell Gina how it cleared up.

GINA: I'll bet it involved Mandy.

SETH: She started bringing home oranges for us.

GINA: Can I ask you guys something? You too, Bernie. You still here?

BERNIE: Here.

GINA: Do you guys think this stuff is admirable?

BERNIE AND SETH:

GENE: I'll handle this, gentlemen. Yes, it is admirable. It is admirable for the same reason that all harmless extremes are, in some way, admirable. The extreme Ultra-Male Behavior is a distillation, a concentrate, wrung from the stuff of ordinary man. It is his essence. It identifies what is uniquely his and elevates it in celebration.

If ordinary male behavior is barley, ultra-male behavior is Johnnie Walker Blue. It is not to everyone's taste, perhaps. Some might find it too strong, even a little harsh. But it is undeniably intoxicating, and there's no gainsaying its quality.

Right, guys?

BERNIE AND SETH: Yeah.

GINA: I don't believe there's anything I could say that could advance my case any more eloquently than you have just done.

SETH: So do I get a prize?

GINA: You want a *prize* for this?

SETH: I thought maybe.

GENE: In fact, there *is* a prize

GINA: Oh, for God's sake.

GENE: You have your choice of two books I have right here. The first is *Merriam-Webster's Collegiate Dictionary.* The second is

How to Good-Bye Depression: If You Constrict Anus 100 Times Every-day. Malarkey? or Effective Way? by Hiroyuki Nishigaki.

SETH: I want that one.

GINA: Big surprise.

BERNIE: Can I have one of those, too?

GENE: No, you didn't win.

GINA: Maybe next time you can park *on top of* another car.

18

Compatibility:
Be Careful with That Match

GENE: We are now going to employ the scientific method to explore a radical and possibly indefensible thesis of mine. My thesis is that if a man is looking to find a woman with whom to share the rest of his life, the best-qualified person to conduct this search—I concede this is a shamefully phallocentric view—is the man. You will not be surprised to know that when I raised this point, Gina disagreed. She said that the man is the *second* most qualified person. The first most qualified person, she said, would be a woman. Any woman.

GINA: That's ridiculous. I didn't say that.

GENE: Yes, you did!

GINA: I said any woman so long as she has known the guy for at least a week and a half.

GENE: True.

GINA: Here is why. Men can be highly intelligent organisms. They can solve complex mathematical equations. However, they do not know *themselves,* because they possess no internal lives.

They are incapable of introspection, and therefore they are incapable of understanding the complexities of relationships, particularly to the extent that these relationships involve themselves and their compatibilities.

I will now demonstrate this for the reader. What is your wife's favorite texture?

GENE: I don't even know what that question means.

GINA: And *your* favorite texture?

GENE: Same answer.

GINA: Okay, now go ask your wife what your favorite texture is.

GENE: Hold on.

GINA: I'm holding.

This will be excellent.

I'm an expert at this sort of thing.

GENE: Back.

GINA: How did it go?

GENE: I had to take notes. She said, "Something coarse and twilled, like denim. If it's leather, it can't have a nap, so suede is out. In wood, you like a strong grain and low gloss, like oak or pine, but not mahogany. In food, you dislike mushy apples but actually seek out mush in pears; otherwise you will eat any texture except gristle, which revolts you. You don't like flannel. You like the feel of freshly laundered sheets but are freaked out and have to leave the room when I smooth them out with the palm of my hand, a reaction that is so weird it's almost psychotic."

GINA: I am guessing this is spot-on?

GENE: Yes.

GENE: And *her* favorite texture?

GENE: I didn't ask.

GINA: Of course not. What's your favorite baseball team?

GENE: The Yankees.

GINA: Who was their third baseman in 1962?

GENE: Cletis Boyer.

GINA: Thank you.

GENE: I fail to see your point.

GINA: My point is that you have a normal male brain, which is in many ways remarkable, capable of retaining amazing minutiae, but that on matters that some might say were important—say, an understanding of yourself—you are without curiosity. It took a woman to reveal and explain them. Same thing with a man's romantic tastes.

GENE: And you are willing to put this up to a test?

GINA: I am. The test we agreed on.

GENE: Okay. We are now each going to sign on to Match.com, a national dating database. It supplies photos and brief autobiographies of women and men looking for relationships. Gina and I are each going to try to find the perfect match for me.

GINA: There are tens of thousands of women here. We have to limit the search. It's possible to restrict it by age and geographical area.

GENE: Let's say we look only within fifty miles of Washington, D.C.

GINA: Fine.

GENE: And between ages thirty and forty-five.

GINA: How old are you?

GENE: Fifty-two.

GINA: Let's say between forty-five and fifty-three.

GENE: I don't think that—

GINA: Put your wife on the phone.

GENE: Okay. Forty-five and fifty-three.

GINA: We will each choose three women.

GENE: Agreed. We meet back here in two hours.

(Two hours pass eventfully. From two hundred possible women, we each chose three, and compared them.)

GENE: I see there are no overlaps.

GINA: Big surprise. Look at the women you picked. This one, the blonde, likes swing dancing. I guess you're quite a hoofer, Crazy Legs.

GENE: Swing dancing? She says that? Where?

GINA: Here. Right near the smiley-face emoticon she ends with.

GENE: I didn't notice that.

GINA: Or how about your second one? The one who thinks it's so interesting that she was born in Cleveland that she puts it in the first five words of her profile?

GENE: Was that the one who looks like Teri Garr?

GINA:

GENE: What?

GINA: You only looked at the pictures, didn't you?

GENE: Physical compatibility is a key element of any relationship.

GINA: I spent two hours reading their profiles!

GENE: Yes, you did. And I have your choices right here, all worthy candidates I would describe as friendly-looking.

GINA: I think they're attractive. You don't find them attractive?

GENE: They're okay. They're not okay enough.

GINA: What does that mean?

GENE: This is something women do not understand. In seeking a mate, men assess women on a complicated sliding scale, with partial credit given in categories such as intelligence, politics, sense of humor, and so forth. But as far as physical appearance, it is pretty much pass-fail. So long as we are talking about a lifetime relationship and not just a night out on the town, a stunningly beautiful supermodel type gets the same passing grade as a woman we find kinda cute.

Every man has his own threshold for "kinda cute." If a woman doesn't make it over the top, other factors are irrelevant. No amount of perkiness or integrity or kindness or smarts can overcome a failing grade in looks. But if she passes, it's a clean slate for everything else. Your women come close but do not pass.

GINA: Those thresholds are not immovable. Love can lower them a great deal.

GENE: So you contend. Now we find out which matchmaking method is better—Gina's, based on a careful calculus of needs and desires as practiced through the millennia by shmatte-bedecked yentas in shtetls—or mine, involving the male system, as practiced most famously by Joey Buttafuoco.

The test took three days. I e-mailed each woman, explaining who I was and that this was a scientific test, not a serious dating inquiry. I asked each to take a ten-question multiple-choice exam to determine compatibility with me. One point for a correct answer. No points for a wrong answer. Sometimes one point was deducted for a *dreadfully* wrong answer.

For example, I asked which trait in a mate would be the biggest turnoff to them: (1) dressing badly, (2) insisting that you take my surname, or (3) using French phrases in ordinary conversation.

The correct answers—the ones that were most compatible with my own turnoffs about people— were (2) and (3). Either answer earned a point. No points were deducted for (1). However, picking the fourth choice lost a point. The fourth choice was: (4) If I showed disrespect and closed-mindedness toward persons with certain New Age beliefs, such as aromatherapy, feng shui, or homeopathy.

GINA: That was the answer your blond swing dancer chose.

GENE: Yes, I see that. None of your women lost a point on that. Two chose correctly, one specifying that if the feng shui thing were true, "I'd marry you on the spot."

The other question that contained a penalty asked the women to arrange my pet names for them in their descending order of preference. Would they rather be called (1) Chipmunk, (2) Sweetiepie, (3) Sluggo, or (4) Bunnygirl. You got one point if you put "Sluggo" first. You lost a point if you put "Sluggo" last.

GINA: Smiley-face lady put "Sluggo" last.

GENE: Yes, she did.

GINA: None of my women did. Two put it first. One said, "I *love* this name!"

GENE: Yes.

GINA: Are we learning something here, Sluggo?

GENE: In fact, only two of my three even deigned to reply, and one of them did it thus: "I really doubt one could find out if another one is compatible with you by having answers to the questions you have prepared below. I find the questions silly and, thus, have opted not to respond."

GINA: Hahahaha. Was that the shrimpy one who looks twelve years old, with no facial expression? The one whose hobby is "staying fit by working out"?

GENE: Yeah. The one with the legs.

GENE: Question five involved the following true news story: A dentist discovered her husband (also a dentist) with another woman. She tore the woman's blouse off, then got in a car and ran her husband over, backing over him twice. As he lay dying, she said to him: "I love you! Keep breathing!" Meanwhile, unbeknown to her, the whole incident was videotaped by a private detective she had hired to follow the husband around. At trial, the videotape became evidence against her.

On my quiz, the women were asked to decide whether this story was (1) tragic, (2) tragic, with some funny aspects, (3) funny, with some tragic aspects, or (4) funny. Gina's women correctly found it a riot. Mine did not.

GINA: What are the final tallies?

GENE: Your women scored 7.5, 7, and 4. Mine scored 3, 0, and 0.

GINA: Point, game, and . . . match.

GENE: Not exactly. You didn't choose the best match possible for me. One other woman took the test.

GINA: Who?

GENE: You.

GINA: Well, sure. You showed me the test, I took it. But—

GENE: I didn't tell you your score.

GINA: No.

GENE: You were the only one who knew that *moist* is a funnier word than *supercalifragilisticexpialidocious*.

GINA: Well, obviously.

GENE: On my compatibility test, you got an 8.

GINA: Hmm.

GENE: Sweetie.

GINA: Put your wife on the phone.

GENE: No.

19

Is Your Relationship Going Anywhere?

GENE: When it comes to vacations, men and women have different but equally valid priorities. Men tend to favor places where adventures occur and opportunities for entertainment present themselves as opposed to places featuring walking tours of historically important catacombs where, in 1742, someone established the first nursing school for Alsatian nuns.

GINA: Oh, please.

GENE: I speak the truth. All men know this.

GINA: Women do not want to be bored on vacations. We want to relax and be pampered, surround ourselves with beauty, and buy things. I don't think there's a huge difference between the sexes here. Most vacations are joint decisions.

GENE: Only to end the nagging or amass critical brownie points toward sexual congress. That's how lounge-in-the-sun vacations happen. By and large, men want adventure.

GINA: In my experience, men mostly want to drive thousands of miles nonstop without conversation, across places like the

Utah desert, which is so mind-numbing and otherworldly that if you saw a triceratops walking across the road, you would simply say, hey, watch out for the damned triceratops.

GENE: Half the *fun* of a vacation is getting there.

GINA: That's like saying half the fun of a bath is filling the tub. Driving may be necessary, but it's not desirable, and the more driving you have to do, the less attractive the final destination becomes. I like an ice-cream sundae, but I'll pass on it if it means I have to milk the cow.

GENE: What do you have against driving?

GINA: For one thing, it introduces an unwelcome element of chance in planning your lodging. You have to take what you can get. On the last such trip, my husband and I found ourselves in a dismal hotel that failed to provide just about everything, including cutlery. So we wound up in a room with nylon sheets, eating potato salad with a shoehorn.

GENE: That sounds interesting!

GINA: My point exactly.

GENE: The single greatest and most memorable event from any vacation I ever had occurred in Mexico's Yucatán Peninsula in 1996, with wife and kids. We realized too late that the VW Bug we had rented had a faulty fuel gauge. I flicked it with my finger, and it dropped from half full to nearly "E." We were sucking fumes on a highway notorious for roving bands of toothless, machete-bearing banditos who robbed you and cut off your head. Exits were about forty miles apart, and most had no gas stations. Man, that was one seriously wired ride. We wound up limping into the airport on an empty tank, pulling up to a rental-car company gas pump, and refusing to move until the attendant gave us a gallon. We settled on $20, American. It was cool.

GINA: That was your most memorable vacation moment?

GENE: Yep. Major league adventure. What's your most memorable vacation moment?

GINA: It happened last summer. We were in Italy at a hotel called Villa d'Este on Lake Como. The hotel had given us a spectacular room with a balcony overlooking the lake. The French doors opened out into the setting sun, with potted plants, beautiful wrought-iron furniture, and complimentary champagne and cheese. It was so lovely and romantic I could have wept, and *then* I found out that Bette Midler was staying in the same hotel and her room wasn't as nice as ours.

GENE: That's not even a *moment*! Nothing happened!

GINA: Well, I admit, it's not a near-death experience. You're way off base here. Men and women both value beauty and serenity, and, above all, romance. Even my husband would agree.

GENE: Really? So if I asked him for his favorite vacation moment, he would say . . .

GINA: Villa d'Este, Italy, balcony, summer 2002, Bette Midler gets aced.

GENE: Put him on the phone.

GINA: Hang on.

GENE: This is going to be enjoyable.

MICHAEL MEYER: Hi.

GENE: Please tell me your all-time favorite vacation moment.

MICHAEL: That's easy. Gina and I were in Colorado, climbing Pikes Peak in a rented SUV . . .

GENE: You listening, Gina?

GINA:

GENE: She's listening.

MICHAEL: Did I say something wrong?

Gene: Not at all! Please continue.

Michael: So Gina gets out at about six-thousand feet, where there's a little outpost selling postcards, but I continue up alone to nine-thousand feet, where it gets pretty hairy. The road is maybe the width of a car and there's a sheer drop on either side. A Chevy Suburban is parked sideways across the road with a hand-lettered sign that says, TURN AROUND, WINDS TOO HIGH. So I'm in this rented SUV, and I don't really know its turning radius, and I have to make a three-point turn. As I'm doing it, I'm hearing gravel tumbling down the cliff. It takes me, literally, fifteen minutes to turn around. It was incredible!

Gina:

Gene: I'm going to hang up now. I'm sure the two of you have lots to talk about.

Gina's List of Women's Favorite Vacation Destinations

Destination	Reason
Milan	shoes
Paris	perfume
New York	jewelry
Hong Kong	fabric
London	silver
Venice	glass
Rio	leather
Bombay	silk
Bozeman, Mont.	boots

Gene's List of Men's Favorite Vacation Destinations

Destination	Reason
Cooperstown, N.Y.	Baseball Hall of Fame
Canton, Ohio	Football Hall of Fame
Springfield, Mass.	Basketball Hall of Fame
St. Louis, Mo.	Bowling Hall of Fame
Cambridge, Mass.	Candlepin Bowling Hall of Fame
Aruba	World's largest miniature golf course
Mattoon, Ill. (late July)	World's largest bagel on parade
City of Rocks, N.M.	Giant rock in shape of toilet
Junction City, Kan.	1800s-era underpants show, modeled by old ladies
Cholame, Calif.	James Dean death-site memorial, consisting of tree wrapped in aluminum in a diner parking lot
Bald Knob, Ark.	Statue of a giant watermelon
Gays, Ill.	A two-story outhouse, *and* a bicycle once ridden by Hitler

Spokane, Wash.	Giant garbage-eating mechanical goat
Tucson, Ariz.	Exhibit of petrified sloth dung
Des Moines, Wash.	Statue of fish with human breasts
Pensacola Beach, Fla.	The Bra Bar, displaying hundreds of customer-donated brassieres
Fountain, Fla.	Roadside zoo with rat-eating frogs

20

Movies: A Disagreement of Cinematic Proportions

GENE: We've known each other for almost two years, but Gina and I didn't go out on our first date until last night. I invited her to the cinema. Because we are not supposed to meet, we attended the same film at the same time—but in different cities. It was a distant but still intimate experience, as with separated lovers contemplating the same moon. And now, it is The Morning After.

Did you have a good time, sweetie?

GINA:

GENE: Doll?

GINA: I cannot believe you took me to that thing.

GENE: It's a box-office *smash!*

GINA: You thought I would like *Jackass: The Movie*?

GENE: Well, I—

GINA: You racked your brains to come up with something we both might appreciate and you decided I am the sort of woman who would enjoy a film so unrelievedly revolting that even the *cameraman* vomits twice. On camera.

GENE: I thought it would give us something to talk about.

GINA:

GENE: Possibly I made an error in judgment.

GINA:

GENE: Let's remain professional about this. We can review it as a team. We'll be just like Siskel and Ebert, if Ebert wore a bra and Siskel weren't dead. And Ebert hated Siskel.

GINA: I don't hate you. I'm just disappointed in you.

GENE: Ow.

GINA: Yeah, well. You want my review?

GENE: Please.

GINA: There are many ways I could have spent my evening more profitably than watching the new release *Jackass: The Movie*. I could, for example, have spent ninety-three minutes sandpapering my tongue. The feebleminded would hesitate to laugh at this movie because it might lower their esteem in the eyes of other half-wits. Had this movie been projected onto cave walls, troglodytes would have turned away in mute shame. Here is comedy at its larval stage, slimy, disgusting, and unformed.

GENE: So that would be a thumb down?

GINA: That would be a thumb in the eyehole of whatever idiot is responsible for this disreputable mess.

GENE: Well, I was offended by it, too.

GINA: You were?

GENE: Yes. It was a relentlessly juvenile string of obnoxious stunts, a movie without plot or purpose other than the celebration of stupidity.

GINA: Exactly.

GENE: So my point is, *thematically* it was fine. But it offended my sense of humor. If a man goes to the radiologist saying he has lower intestinal pain but does not know why, you definitely should not first show how he deliberately created the cause of his discomfort. It ruins the otherwise excellent joke when it turns out, on the X ray, to be a Matchbox car up his gazoo.

If you are going to have a near-naked man tightrope-walk over a pit of alligators with a dead chicken dangling from his jockstrap, do it right. You want the guy to keep his balance long enough to create some tension and suspense. Plus, you don't want the chicken to keep falling off—that's just sloppy. You want it securely attached, such as with braided galvanized wire crimped by no. 2 ferrule bolts.

GINA: You disliked this movie because of *production values?*

GENE: And intellectual lassitude. The execution was flawed. The concept —by which I mean jerks grossing each other out for the simple joy of sedition—was sound. It was a barometer of the culture of our times.

GINA: A rectal barometer. I fail to see how a man kicking himself in the forehead, or trampolining into a spinning ceiling fan, or eating a urine sno-cone, or snorting a line of wasabi until he hurls on the sushi bar qualifies as a concept, let alone a sound concept.

GENE: Maybe it's a guy thing. I accept that you did not like this movie, and I apologize for taking you to it. Will you go out with me again?

GINA: Maybe.

GENE: Please.

GINA: If I pick the movie.

GENE: That's fine with me.

GINA: It won't be.

GENE: Uh-oh.

GENE: Okay, we're back. We will now review Gina's movie selection, which was the Truffaut classic *The Story of Adele H.* We each watched it on video.

GINA: Set in the 1860s, this is a tale of unrequited love in which a vulnerable young Frenchwoman is driven to the edge of sanity and beyond by her romantic obsession for a British soldier who seduced and then abandoned her. She follows him from Europe to Canada to try to persuade him to do the honorable thing and marry her.

GENE: Set in the 1860s, this is a tale of a man pursued by a wack job.

GINA: Constrained by the hypocritical standards of a society that punishes women for behavior tolerated in men, Adele finds herself robbed of her only negotiable quality, her virginity. Thus, when confronted by her ex-lover's coldness and cadlike rebuffs, she employs increasingly desperate and self-abasing measures to win him back and restore her honor.

GENE: Wack. Job.

GINA: She begins by beseeching him, but when he remains callously unmoved by her entreaties, she resorts to stealth, duplicity, and coercion.

GENE: If he'd owned a rabbit, she'd have boiled it.

GINA: *The Story of Adele H.* is an emotional drama of almost unendurable passion and intensity.

GENE: Nothing much happens.

GINA: In setting the movie among French expatriates in North America, the filmmaker deftly contrasts sensibilities of disparate cultures.

GENE: Half the film is in English and half in French, deftly ensuring that no matter where it is shown, the audience will have to slog through subtitles.

GINA: The pacing is elegantly restrained.

GENE: Virtually every scene ends with someone staring wistfully into the middle distance. At one point, we watch Adele agonizing for two full screen minutes about which dress to wear. Another scene consists entirely of Adele, in her bedroom, mournfully worshiping at a shrine to her lover. This lasts one minute and three seconds, during which time the only action—indeed, the only perceptible motion—involves a single teardrop inching down her cheek.

GINA: The cinematography masterfully accentuates gloom and foreboding, evoking a disconsolate mood through the use of shadow and oblique lighting.

GENE: The entire movie appears to have been filmed at dusk. To achieve maximum inscrutability, most of the scenes take place in garrets and attics, seemingly inside closets and under beds, shot through a lens covered by dust bunnies. All the clothing is brown.

GINA: It stars the beautiful Isabelle Adjani in a breathtaking performance.

GENE: Wait. That's not Winona Ryder?

GINA: It's Isabelle Adjani. *The Story of Adele H.* was made in 1975, when Winona Ryder was a four-year-old named Winona Horowitz. She was probably shoplifting Pampers.

GENE: Well, I am not convinced.

GINA: Well, you are an idiot.

GENE: The film betrays a serious failure on the part of the director in that Winona/Isabelle's beauty is, in fact, still evident—despite Truffaut's heroic measures to disguise this vulgar fact by hiding her under bustles, bonnets, shawls, and dresses that seem to be fashioned from brocaded bedspreads. The steamiest scene occurs when a lovesick bookseller looks out the window and is fevered by the sight of a clothesline from which is hanging Adele's underwear. They resemble clown pants.

GINA: Based upon the true story of novelist Victor Hugo's troubled second daughter, the film conveys an authentic feel by relying heavily on epistolary records.

GENE: About a quarter of the movie consists of Adele scowling furiously as she reads aloud from letters she is writing.

GINA: The dialogue is spare and intense.

GENE: The dialogue is as treacly as sap, and as sappy as treacle. Here's an actual sample: "It was *you* who sought me out. *You* who furtively touched my arm. *You* who caressed me in the corridor. Before we part forever, tell me that you could still love me."

GINA: Adele represents the most extreme version of what the ordinary woman feels when hopelessly in love, obedient to no laws of logic or order, a state where all previous guidelines for behavior are up for reevaluation, where one's self-worth and dignity cannot compete with a blind and irrational need to own and be owned, in body and soul, by another. There is something pathetic about Adele, but something noble, too; in the grandeur of her pain and the almost eager way she embraces her own humiliation, we feel a common human experience. Ultimately, this film is about every woman.

GENE: Ultimately, this film is about every wack job.

21

Bathroom Humor

GENE: One casualty of the twentieth-century sexual revolution is that men and women have become less of a mystery to each other. In Elizabethan times, men spoke to women far differently: Intergender communication required an entire vocabulary of euphemism and formality, involving words like "prithee." Women never wore trousers. Men always handled the money. Women could not fix oxcarts and men could not fix dinners, and each remained awed by, and respectful of, the other's skills.

GINA: You contend that Elizabethan-era men were "respectful of" women's skills?

GENE: That's probably not the perfect expression.

GINA: Correct. The perfect expression would be "dismissive of." Or "patronizing toward." Or "content to be serviced by."

GENE: I will retract that characterization. Let's leave it that men and women didn't understand much about each other's lives. There was mystery. Now, all has changed. Now, husbands and wives talk plainly. Women operate forklifts. Men do the laundry. More often than not, women control the checkbook. At the supermarket, men are compelled to purchase feminine hygiene products. Men are under intense social pressure to pretend to be grateful for the opportunity to observe, in gynecological detail, the Miracle of Birth, with the attendant vomitaceous thrashings and squirtations.

In short, today men and women work and live side by side, intimate in ways romantic and banal, almost functionally indistinguishable. This is true except for the one place they remain apart, the one place where mysteries of gender may still be plumbed. The bathroom.

GINA: I wondered where you were going with this.

GENE: I am going where no man has gone before. The ladies' room.

GINA: Dangerous territory, cowboy.

GENE: Stand back, I'm goin' in.

GINA: Nothing so terrifies the sexes as the threat of an incursion into each other's privies. The Equal Rights Amendment, one of the least threatening or offensive documents ever put up to a public referendum, failed mostly because conservatives managed to gleefully sprinkle the idiotic notion across much of bucktoothed America that its passage would inevitably lead to communal bathrooms.

GENE: You'd think men wouldn't have minded all that much.

GINA: Men don't want to appear vulnerable in the eyes of women. Women don't want to appear undignified in the eyes of men. A bathroom stall confers vulnerability and robs dignity. The Ally McBeal bathroom exists only in fiction.

GENE: Whatever the reason, each sex remains ignorant about this aspect of the other. A few years ago I learned something about women that poleaxed me. My family and I had just returned from a vacation in London, where persons seated on the wrong side of the car drive on the wrong side of the road. I mentioned that I had found this disorienting, but less disorienting than the toilets. My wife and daughter asked what I meant.

Hadn't they noticed? I reminded them that the flush handle on the toilets was on the opposite side from what we are used to. You have to reach back with your left hand, I said, instead of your right.

GINA: Your right *hand?*

GENE: That is exactly what my wife said, and exactly the inflection with which she said it.

GINA: Well, of course.

GENE: Please tell every single male reader, to his astonishment, exactly what my wife and daughter then informed me

GINA: They informed you that in public bathrooms, they flush with their feet.

GENE: You got it.

GINA: Virtually all women flush with their feet. A small subset use their elbows.

GENE: So testified my wife and daughter. My son and I regarded each other with amazement. It was as though we had just been told that, say, Norwegians have three buttocks.

GINA: Are you actually telling me men use their *hands?* In *public bathrooms?*

GENE: Absolutely.

GINA: That's disgusting. The thing is filthy.

GENE: You're *supposed* to handle it. Why do you think they call it a handle?

GINA: If they called it a mouthle, would you lick it? I fail to believe most men use their hands.

GENE: And men fail to believe most women *don't* use their hands. Most men are shocked, even men who should know.

ALEXANDER KIRA: I have to confess this is the first time I've heard this.

GINA: Who are you?

GENE: Gina, meet Dr. Kira. He is a retired professor of architecture at Cornell University. In 1976 he wrote a book called *The Bathroom,* which remains the definitive work on the subject. Didn't know it at all, Doc?

DR. KIRA: Not until this second. But you know, it makes sense. I had not factored in immediately the flush valve, which is what is used in most commercial bathrooms. It is lower to the ground and easier to kick. Couple that with the fact that one of the common behaviors for women in most places is not to sit down. They hover.

GENE: They hover?

GINA: Yes. In particularly grungy conditions, we hover.

DR. KIRA: You see, contact is the number one issue for women.

GENE: Ha ha. Pun intended?

DR. KIRA: Ah, no.

GENE: Okay, thanks, Doc.

GINA: So far we have established only that you and some guy at Cornell use your hands.

GENE: It's universal. I confirmed it with Bob Giese, whose title is senior human factors analyst at the Kohler Company, the omnibus toilet manufacturer in Kohler, Wisconsin. Though a man, Bob has done extensive field studies. Most women, he said, flush with their feet. When I asked him if men do, too, he said "some" men, the way one might say that "some" men enjoy the company of sheep. The large majority of men, he said, use their hands. It is why there are more plumbing repairs needed in women's public bathrooms. Kicking is harder on the fixtures.

What we learn from this, once again, tiresome as this fact may be becoming, is that Darwin was right. This is the Galapagos, right here.

GINA: The Galapagos?

GENE: Modern men and women may have grown more and more alike over the years, through greater familiarity with each other. But in the one place they are forever kept apart—on separate islands, like the tortoises of the Galapagos—they have been free to develop distinct and eccentric patterns of behavior, uninfluenced by each other. Mothers pass bathroom conventions on to their daughters, fathers to their sons. And so we have the flushing anomaly. Plus, who knows what else.

GINA: I don't intend to frequent men's rooms to find out. My curiosity is not that great. On the rare occasions when I have been forced by circumstance to use a men's room, it was unoccupied and I had a sentry positioned outside. On those occasions, I managed to be as quick as possible and look neither left nor right. What I saw was bad enough. What I smelled was worse. What is it with you guys and basic hygiene?

GENE: I will admit that our standards are not as high.

GINA: Your standards are nonexistent.

GENE: We understand that it is a dysfunction. Case in point: One day many years ago—in fact, it was August 11, 1991—my wife and I were at a baseball game with our friends Joel Achenbach and Mary Stapp, and their three-month-old daughter, Paris. It was at the stately old home of the Baltimore Orioles, Memorial Stadium. *Stately* is a word that sportswriters, intoxicated by the so-called romance of baseball, employ to describe a stadium of infinite decrepitude. Memorial Stadium was a dump.

On that day, something remarkable was happening on the field. An unknown pitcher for the Chicago White Sox, a rookie left-hander named Wilson Alvarez, was throwing a no-hitter against the then-mighty Orioles. It was in the late innings and it was therefore essential that Joel and I watch every second of what was going on. We had to carefully marshal and synchronize our bathroom time.

Well, we suddenly found ourselves with a precious three minutes between innings. But neither Mary nor my wife was around. You know women: They were probably off shopping for Orioles jogging bras or something. So Joel had no choice but to strap Paris into one of those Snugli thingies, like a backpack that hangs on your chest, and take her with us.

So there we were in a Memorial Stadium restroom, standing side by side at one of those trough urinals.

GINA: What is a trough urinal?

GENE: It is like a long, skinny bathtub. Guys just sort of waddle up to it and unzip.

GINA: There is no separation between you? No little privacy wall?

GENE: No, there is no "little privacy wall."

GINA: I don't know what to say. I seriously do not know what to say.

GENE: Say nothing. This is my story.

GINA: The whole urinal thing is very disturbing to women.

GENE: It is very practical. It is also timeless. In ancient Hebrew versions of the Bible, the term for "man" is *mashtin bekir*, which translates roughly into "one who pisseth against a wall."

Anyway, Joel and I are standing next to each other in a room so humid with the stench of recycled beer that we are like two little decorative ceramic frogmen at the bottom of a urine aquarium. Beneath us is a sloshing bathtub, its drains clogged with cigarette butts. Sweet little Paris is looking worshipfully up at her daddy's face, her legs dangling a foot or two over this cesspool.

Joel and I are sort of eyeing each other uncomfortably. Not a word has passed between us since we entered the place. It is a mission. We have to do what we have to do, and we both know it.

Finally, Joel says, "Gene?"

"Yeah?" I say, zipping up manfully.

Joel zips, too.

"Mary never needs to find out about this."

"Agreed," I say solemnly. And she never did.

GINA: Until she reads this.

GENE: The statute of limitations expired last year. Paris is a beautiful, well-adjusted young lady. Evidently she wasn't scarred.

GINA: No thanks to you guys.

GENE: You probably want to know what happened in the game.

GINA: I don't give a damn what happened in the game.

GENE: Alvarez completed the no-hitter, thanks to a shoestring catch by the right fielder.

GINA: Wonderful.

GENE: I seem to be doing all the talking. It's time you shared.

GINA: Shared what?

GENE: Secrets from the loo.

GINA: No, thank you.

GENE: You took money from Simon & Schuster. Now you have to put out.

GINA:

GENE: You are contractually obligated.

GINA: There's a great deal of flushing.

GENE: Huh?

GINA: In a ladies' room. A significant amount of flushing goes on. You flush before you sit down.

GENE: What? Why?

GINA: Because it's fresher that way.

GENE: But the previous person flushed.

GINA: There could be lingering pee molecules. You can't be too careful. So you flush before. And you flush after.

GENE: Well, of course you flush after.

GINA:

GENE: What?

GINA: And in between.

GENE: In between? Why?

GINA: Sound camouflage.

GENE: Men don't do that.

GINA: Big surprise.

GENE: I thought women were great environmentalists.

GINA: Not on the toilet.

GENE: On the toilet you are content to drain the oceans?

GINA: Yes.

GENE: Why is this like pulling teeth?

GINA: I am not really enjoying it.

GENE: I am.

GINA: I know.

GENE: Actually, the sound thing is an international obsession among women. Japanese women have been known to make themselves sick with constipation because they don't want their husbands to hear them in the bathroom. There is a product marketed to women in Japan called the Sound Princess. It's basically a tape deck that you switch on when you sit down, and it makes nice, pleasant nature noises like birds chirping and brooks babbling.

Wouldn't it be a great practical joke to sneak in and alter the tape so that every fifteen minutes or so the Sound Princess emitted an earsplitting fart?

GINA: Are we almost through with this chapter?

GENE: Not quite. We need to exit on something really strong. Besides, I don't have a clear enough picture of the . . . I don't know . . . the *ambience* in a woman's bathroom. There is a lot of flushing and primping, then?

GINA: Right. Beaucoup mirrors.

GENE: Anything else? You may remain monosyllabic, if you wish.

GINA: Talk.

GENE: Talk?

GINA: Yes.

GENE: Women talk?

GINA: Yes.

GENE: Stall to stall? With strangers?

GINA: Not all women do, but enough so it is not at all uncommon.

GENE: What sort of talk?

GINA: "I bought six nice throw pillows on sale. Second floor, housewares." "Ooh, thanks, I'll head right up there." "I'm gonna leave them on that son of a bitch's couch so he'll have something else to put his hands on other than the tramp next door, because I'm out of there." "Tell me about it. It sounds like my first marriage. . . ."

GENE: This is while peeing?

GINA: Right.

GENE: That's amazing.

GINA: Men don't talk?

GENE: Seldom at the urinal, never in the stalls. Have you ever seen a dog that is approached by another dog while it is hunched in the poop position? Teeth are bared. It's an extremely vulnerable moment—ancient, feral reflexes swing into play. Men do not want their privacy breached while helpless; there may be some unattractive homophobia lurking in this, but I think it is more your basic wolf defense.

If a guy starts talking to me from the next stall, unless it is to alert me he is having a heart attack, I shoot first and ask questions later. All you need is one male out of the twelve and, worst-case scenario, the jury is hung.

GINA: You said "hung."

GENE: That's crude.

GINA: I'm going with the flow.

GENE: All I'm trying to say is that if you are in a public men's room, it does not matter how many pants are down around how many ankles—you do not talk. Unless you consider bodily sounds "speech," in which case you are voluble and unrestrained.

GINA: I doubt anyone would define farting as speech.

GENE: The United States Supreme Court probably would. They consider lots of stuff to be speech. Flag burning is speech. So are campaign contributions. Farting isn't much of a stretch.

GINA: Back up a minute. You said "pants around ankles."

GENE: Yes?

GINA: Men drop their pants to their ankles?

GENE: Women don't?

GINA: *You let your pants touch the filthy floor?*

GENE: I guess. If it's loose material. How would you prevent it?

GINA: By any means necessary! You spread your thighs to hold them at your knees.

GENE: Women do this?

GINA: Every woman on the face of the earth. Men don't?

GENE: No man on the face of the earth.

GINA: Your pants dangle into the filth.

GENE: I suppose.

GINA: I'm never giving head again.

GENE: Whoa!

GINA: Can we be done with this chapter, please?

GENE: *Now* we can, babe.

22

C'mon, Baby—
What Are You Afraid Of?

GENE: I have a theory about human behavior. It might help explain the most profound differences between men and women.

GINA: Does it involve either underpants or bathroom activities?

GENE: You injure me. I am not a vulgarian.

GINA:

GENE: It involves a cattle prod up the arse.

GINA: Thank you. Proceed.

GENE: Behavioral scientists discovered long ago that although a monkey will learn to perform a trick for a banana, under proper conditions he can learn it much faster to avoid an electric shock to a sensitive area. What may we conclude from this?

GINA: We may conclude that behavioral scientists are men. Women do not use cattle prods. With women, punishment involves stern expressions of disapproval or, if absolutely necessary, time-outs. If the monkeys were insufficiently motivated by a banana, women scientists would have diced it up into a nice fruit salad.

GENE: Noted. However, the scientists were men and we are left with their data. We can conclude from it, I think, that the things we *fear* in life influence our behavior and shape our personality to a greater degree than the things we *want*. These fears are customized: Everyone has a different thing that terrifies him more than anything else. This thing, whatever it may be, is so scary that our natural impulse is not to confront it, but to wallpaper over it.

GINA: Not men. Men hate wallpaper.

GENE: Stop interrupting.

GINA: I am pointing out a flaw in your logic. Women love wallpaper because it offers almost infinite choice. You can choose pretty designs. It's like putting a party dress on your house. Men hate wallpaper for the same reason they have suits in twelve shades of gray. To decorate their homes, men like to apply paint with six-foot-long rollers, a vast acreage of neutral colors. Women, on the other hand, understand that wallpaper offers a little *frisson*. The possibilities are limitless and your only rule is to avoid anything with repeating images of small animals. I lean toward William Morris prints from the Victoria and Albert Museum.

GENE:

GINA: All right, go ahead with your little theory.

GENE: No, you ruined it.

GINA: Oh, for heaven's sake, don't be such a baby. I'm with you so far. You are trying to say that we disguise and deny our fears the way we would try to hide a hole in the wall.

GENE: It's more like a lump on the wall. An unattractive nugget of fear. Logically, we should confront it directly, sand it down, spackle the rough spots, and be done with it. But we don't. We go for the wallpaper. And we choose a design as unlike what's underneath as possible. Then we spend the rest of our lives trying to iron out the lump as best we can. After a while, everyone else sees only the wallpaper. They think that's what we really are, but it's not—it's precisely the opposite, a denial of what we really are.

At his core, the redneck bigot doesn't really feel superior to others. He is someone who cannot confront the knowledge, deep down, that he and others like him are critically deficient in talent and ability and doomed to a marginal life. The religious zealot is someone who might well lose his mind if he had to face his very strong and petrifying suspicion that he is out there all alone. I'm painfully shy to the point of disability, so I have chosen a career in which I make a fool of myself as often and as publicly as possible.

GINA: Believe it or not, I'm still with you.

GENE: You are?

GINA: I am. This unusual condition has lasted an entire eight paragraphs. We should break out the bubbly. You want to analyze the differences between men and women by confronting the things we most fear.

GENE: Yes. What do women most fear?

GINA: Men.

GENE: No, really.

GINA: Really. Girls are taught from an early age that they are uniquely vulnerable to bad men with bad intentions. Comic Elayne Boosler said she once declined to go out walking at night because she felt she made too easy a target: "Unfortunately," she said, "I was wearing nice jewelry, and a handbag, and I had my vagina on me. . . ."

Our biology sets us up as victims. Across every jurisdiction on the planet there exists an entire category of crime that, physiologically speaking, can be perpetrated only by a man on a woman. Our mothers remind us of this from the time we are old enough to be out on our own. You know how menstruating women are not supposed to swim in the ocean because sharks will get them? Mom informs us this is nothing compared with the threat of the dreaded hammerhead land shark, who smells blood always. Fear is a matriarchal inheritance. In return, we are granted the ability to wear pink and demand attention, and we are granted the license to cry without guilt or apology. What do men most fear?

GENE: Crying.

GINA: No, really.

GENE: Really. Men do not, elementally, fear being victimized. We fear losing control. We fear losing emotional control and proving ourselves weak in front of others. We don't want you to see us cry. In fact, seeing *you* cry renders us all fidgety and helpless because we are unable to control a loss of control in others.

But more important, we fear losing *physical* control of our lives. We fear powerlessness. Men don't fear being raped nearly as much as we fear being forced to watch the rape of our women and being powerless to stop it.

Want to know the nightmare I most frequently have, the one that can wake me with the sweats? I am at the controls of a small plane. My family is there, and their lives are in my hands, and I realize to my horror that I do not know how to land.

GINA: I have something to tell you that you are not going to believe, but I can prove it.

GENE: Of course I'll believe you. We're partners.

GINA: My most common nightmare involves being a passenger in a plane that is being piloted by a man who does not know how to land.

GENE: I don't believe you.

GINA: I wrote about it twenty years ago, in a personal journal I keep. It's on my computer. I have just copied it, pasted it, and am e-mailing you right now.

CHEERFUL MALE BARITONE: You've got mail!

GINA: Did I have time to write it as we were talking?

GENE: No.

GINA: Don't read it. Copy it and paste it onto this page.

The plane-over-the-cityscape dream again: I'm in first class, feeling good for a change. The weather is clear and I am surprised—suspicious, maybe a little—by a lack of the usual, relentless paralyzing fear of being in a plane. I am looking out the window and see that we are beginning our descent. I keep hoping to see a runway but all I see are city streets, buildings. We are practically flying between them and I know we will soon clip one with a wing, how could we not? I am terrified and want to scream but don't want to make other people feel worse than they already do. The captain is saying nothing. He is not homicidal, he is incompetent. The sky is still blue. The buildings are a few feet away, and drawing closer. Being in first class no longer makes a difference.

GENE: Whoa.

GINA: What do you make of this?

GENE: A man's fear is worse, because guilt is added. In my dream, I'm the one at fault.

GINA: Wrong. Women's fear is worse, because yours is rectifiable. You can learn to pilot your plane. Your fear permits you hope. Mine allows none. It is ultimate despair. And do you know why that is?

GENE: I am guessing it is because of the overall condition of womanhood, caused by some terrible gender inequity in our society, fostered by men's arrogance and hostility, a situation plain to you but unknown to me because men prefer to keep themselves ignorant of facts that tend to portray them in a bad light.

GINA: Good, good. You are learning.

Girls are not taught or encouraged to slough off their fears and anxieties, or to battle their enemies and demons directly. We are not taught to think of ourselves as pilots or fighters. Part of the reasoning behind this is perfectly adaptive to the real world of the playground—a girl who punches, even when she punches her enemy in defense, will be regarded as deviant in a way that a boy will not.

Girls are often encouraged to maintain their neediness instead of forging their own sets of strengths. They are encouraged to look for protection from their parents and family, and to transfer this desire to a lover or husband as they grow into adulthood. The winners are the ones who never have to face their fears directly.

It is that old matriarchal line of fear. My grandmother—my mother's mother—was irrationally afraid of thunderstorms. Whenever she was alone in one, caught at home without her husband, she would drag my mother and her six brothers and sisters through the driving rain to the house of a neighbor, where they would sit under the neighbor's thrumming tin roof. Because of her fear of facing her fear alone, she would bring everyone to a house that was, in essence, an echo chamber, potentiating her terror like alcohol on top of barbiturates. She may as well have gone outside with a kite and a key. She was a woman. She drank deep of her fears.

The maternal line is strong. Early in my dating youth, I had a relationship that wasn't working, and I could not face my fear that it was over—because if I thought that he didn't love me, the entire infrastructure of my life at that time would have collapsed under the slightest pressure, like the stairs in a haunted house. Now, what would a typical man do if he was afraid his relationship was breaking up and didn't want it to happen?

GENE: He would work his darnedest to win his sweetheart back through greater sensitivity and improved communication, so that he might better understand her needs and dedicate himself to satisfying them.

GINA:

GENE: He would stalk her.

GINA: Precisely. Unstable, unwise, immature, and hostile, but inarguably decisive. Women tend not to think this way. With this boyfriend, I remained entirely passive but pathetically needy. I remember getting a postcard from him and trying to squeeze reassurance from the fact that he signed the message "Love."

Now, ending a communication with "love" is nearly reflexive with me—I have to stop myself from putting it above my signature on a tax return—but there I was, gripping this poor little word at the bottom of his grubby postcard, trying to wring some juice out of it, like trying to get milk from a stone. We split up shortly afterward.

GENE: Your point is?

GINA: My point is that you are right that men and women alter our personalities to try to cope with our most elemental fears. Since men fear losing control, they spend their lives trying for it, which makes them aggressive, competitive, and comparatively emotionless. Women see themselves, down deep, as victims of forces beyond our control, and so we react not by fighting our fears or denying them but by internalizing them and adapting to them the best we can. It makes us more complex.

GENE: It certainly does.

GINA: What is that supposed to mean?

GENE: Nothing.

GINA: You are defining "complex" as "neurotic"?

GENE: If the shoe fits . . .

GINA: This is an example of the typical, infuriating male sense of superiority.

GENE: That's where you are wrong. Men do not feel superior to women.

GINA: Oh, please.

GENE: Really. Deep down, a man believes that women are better than he is in almost every way. This fills him with no small amount of wonder. He is genuinely puzzled by the fact that his woman can bring herself to love something as lumpy and ugly as he is, and that she will actually sleep with him. *He* wouldn't sleep with him.

He is stunned by how this smaller person can exercise such power over him, and that she not only knows that camel and burgundy go together nicely, whatever that means, and knows intuitively where every department is located in a department store even if she has never been there before, and can tell you the age of every child she sees on the street, sometimes to the month—not only all that, but that she can also stop time and all logical thought whenever she feels like it by simply placing her tongue in his mouth.

But beneath his awe—and it is a genuine awe—he has this nagging belief, approaching certitude, that women are, despite their inarguably wonderful qualities and competencies, completely out of their minds.

So yeah, neurotic.

GINA: It is not neurosis, it is complexity. Men and women both know fear, but women are much more intimately familiar with it. Fear confers timidity. Fear looks both ways but still refuses to cross; fear looks twice and still doesn't leap. Fear believes that the early worm gets caught by the bird.

This is what women live with, in much greater numbers than men do. We all deal with it, and many of us, even most of us, transcend it. But it is not easy.

GENE: What's the secret?

GINA: We have various techniques. For example, we are adept at casually distributing some fears to men so that ours don't stand out in such sharp relief.

GENE: What sort of fears?

GINA: Little things that gnaw at you.

GENE: Such as?

GINA: It's better not to dwell on it. You guys have enough to worry about, what with all your manly duties. You don't need to know that the best orgasms your women have are self-administered.

GENE: *What?*

GINA: Whoopsie.

23

It's the Money, Honey
(Part I—The Challenge)

GINA: Why are men so secretive about money?

GENE: We aren't.

GINA: How much do you make?

GENE:

GINA: See?

GENE: How much do *you* make?

GINA: My salary as an English professor is $84,000. My speaker's fee is between $3,500 and $5,000, and I average at least one speaking engagement a month. Your turn.

GENE:

GINA: This is so typical of men. A few years ago, I was watching some actor being interviewed on TV. He was really opening up about his years of tawdry, indiscriminate sexual relations and providing every disgusting detail. It seemed a pathetic search for validation by a pitiably needy man whose narcissism seemed to hide an insecurity bordering on self-loathing. And finally, the interviewer changed the subject. She said, "Okay, let's talk about your new film. You're getting $3 million—right?" And his face gets all pinched, and he says he's not going to discuss money. Too private.

What *is* it with you guys?

GENE: I think it's natural not to want to discuss income, because when you do, you seem to be either bragging or complaining. Plus, whatever the numbers, you become an object of idiotic gossip and debate. People you barely know will subject your professional worth to a cost-benefit analysis. No, men don't discuss money. I think it's weird that women do.

GINA: Women discuss *everything*. Haven't you figured that out yet? But money in particular is no big deal. It's because we're still pretty new at being in control of our own finances. We find money fascinating. We like dealing with it. We like handling it.

GENE: Is that why women will stand at the cashier at the front of a long line in a crowded lunchroom and fumble in their purses for two minutes looking for exact change while everyone else's soup gets cold?

GINA: No. That is because women have *feelings* for economically oppressed and marginalized people, such as cashiers, who appreciate change because they are always running out. Whereas a man will blithely present a twenty for a seventy-nine-cent purchase so as not to have to calculate change, which will give him more time to calculate the odds that the cashier will sleep with him, which happen to be zero, because just look at that gut on him.

The fact is, women are historically comfortable with small change, because it is what we've been told to live with most of our lives. As recently as twenty years ago, the only money that women typically carried was "pin money" or "mad money." Money for women was thought of as something for trivialities and incidentals, usually apportioned to us as an "allowance." It's still true, to some degree.

GENE: Not in my house. In my house, my wife handles the cash.

GINA: That's unusual.

GENE: It's unavoidable. I am absentminded, irresponsible, and impractical.

For a short period in my life in my mid-twenties, I lived alone. I would remember to pay the electric bill every month only after the power went out for nonpayment. Going dark was my tickler file. One morning a month, I had to run over to the utility company and pay in cash. The clerks would laugh.

I would remember to feed my dog only when she came up to me, around nine o'clock every night, and basically pointed to her mouth. I would never have any dog food around, so I had to run out to the convenience store, and because I never had any cash around, either, I could only buy one can of food. This ritual repeated the following night.

GINA: No wonder you married the dog food lady.

GENE: Exactly. I am still basically this same comically dysfunctional person, and she and I know it and we make the necessary accommodations. For example, I am not permitted to carry a checkbook, because for one to have a checkbook and not go to prison, it is necessary to keep a record of what checks one has written, which I could never do. Therefore, my wife issues me one check at a time, which I keep in my wallet. I am like Barney Fife, the incompetent sheriff's deputy on the old *Andy Griffith Show*, who was issued only one bullet.

GINA: I don't think your home situation is related to money. I think it's related to your being a nincompoop.

GENE: Agreed.

GINA: In fact, though women are less secretive about money, I think we are more intimidated by it. I do think that, in general, men are more comfortable *dealing* with money than women are. You don't need to look any further than the amusing scene that results after a group of ladies of a certain age go to lunch and the check arrives. A check should be split with an axe, the way men do, and not with little pinking shears and manicure scissors. Slowly, women are learning this.

However, just because men are more comfortable with money doesn't mean they are better with money. They are not.

GENE: I guess that's why all the Wall Street tycoons are women.

GINA: So you think men are better investors?

GENE: I bet they are.

GINA: Wrong. Bad investment. Pay up.

In 1998, the University of California, Davis, did a study of women's behavior in the stock market and concluded that women tend to be more successful investors than men. It's not that women pick better stocks—they don't. It's that they pick *fewer* stocks. They stick with their decisions and remain loyal to the companies they choose.

Men, on the other hand, tend to trade and trade. They will swagger around, trusting their own instincts and hunches even when their instincts are unsound and their hunches are wrong. Because the stock market is essentially a crapshoot, they will make money sometimes and lose money sometimes—roughly proportional to the women—but because they are so trigger-happy, they will make more trades, meaning they will spend more in commissions, meaning they will lose more overall.

It is exactly like dating and marriage. In stock trading, men are more promiscuous than women, and they wind up paying through the nose for the privilege of screwing around.

GENE: Interesting. But men are better negotiators, which is what commerce is really all about.

GINA: Men are not better negotiators.

GENE: Yes, we are. It is because, in matters of money, men are ruthless. Women don't want to hurt feelings. They don't have it in their guts to be ruthless.

GINA: Yes, we do.

GENE: Have you ever seen a woman try to buy a car? I have. From a commercial standpoint, it isn't pretty.

My wife, who negotiates criminal plea agreements mercilessly for the United States government, will walk into a showroom, find the car she wants, get real excited, and inform the salesman that she must have *THIS* car, *RIGHT NOW,* that *NO OTHER CAR WILL DO,* and then, um, ask the price. I may not be permitted to have a checkbook, but she is not permitted to open her mouth during a business transaction.

GINA: I can get a better price on a car than you can.

GENE: You cannot.

GINA: Yes, I can.

GENE: You would be willing to put this to a test?

GINA: What kind of test?

GENE: We go buy the same car. Different dealerships, different cities, but the identical car with the identical accessories. Low price wins.

GINA: I pick the car.

GENE: What difference does it make what car it is?

GINA: I want a nice car.

GENE: Um, we're not actually buying it. We back out after we get the final sale price.

GINA: I don't care. You picked the test, I pick the car.

GENE: Okay.

GINA: A Mercedes S500. Black.

GENE: That's ridiculous. I would feel uncomfortable even *pretending* to buy a Mercedes.

GINA: Why?

GENE: Mercedeses are for pretentious oinkers.

GINA: I drive a Mercedes.

GENE: Pretentious oinkers and lovely, intriguing women.

GINA: What do *you* drive, Gomer?

GENE: I drive a 1991 Mazda 323, which is the size of a Saint Bernard. It is so filled with junk that I once found in the backseat, under a mound of two-year-old newspapers, an uneaten take-out chicken dinner. It had fossilized, stinkless within its Styrofoam coffin. Once, when I went to get this car inspected, the inspector refused to get in. He gave me a lecture on proper car hygiene. This was a guy whose hair looked like it had been styled with a pomade of Valvoline and soot.

My point is, I would like to buy a car more consistent with my persona.

GINA: We are not going to buy a Little Tikes Cozy Coupe.

GENE: How about an SUV?

GINA: I will be taken for a suburban matron and disrespected. I want a Mercedes S500.

GENE: How about compromising on a sports car?

GINA: I will be taken for a poseur and disrespected. I want a Mercedes S500.

GENE: You're not negotiating.

GINA: Yes, I am. If you want to do the test, we will buy a Mercedes.

GENE:

GINA: That is my negotiating stance.

GENE: Okay.

GINA: Good.

GENE: I don't think I like the way this is starting out.

GINA: I do.

24

It's the Money, Honey
(Part II—The Test)

GENE: Are you back?

GINA: Yep.

GENE: Did you get a good price?

GINA: Yep.

GENE: You sound pretty confident.

GINA: Yep.

GENE: Well, I guarantee that you did not beat my price.

GINA: Don't be too sure.

GENE: I am sure, and here is why: This test involves the deployment of two quintessentially male weapons. The first is negotiation, at which men excel. The second involves the very nature of this enterprise, which is a competition. Men are insanely competitive, particularly where there is a simple win-lose goal. Women are different.

My friend Pat was playing a set of tennis with a friend of hers recently. Pat had fallen behind early but staged a furious comeback, and the two women were knotted at 6–6. Good game, nice long volleys. They were both elated at how exciting it had been. What do you think happened next?

GINA: They hugged and went home.

GENE: Yes! Yes, that is *exactly* what they did! They were both pumped and excited, and they didn't want either one to feel bad about losing such a thrilling match, so they quit at a tie. Two men would not quit at a tie if they came under mortar attack. You must have a winner. You must have a loser. You must have license to gloat.

Women simply do not have this killer instinct.

GINA: Are you finished?

GENE: Yes.

GINA: This is not tennis. Tennis is frivolity. Friendly athletic competitions have no meaning, except to men, who—for reasons involving extreme ego impairment—invest them with preposterously disproportionate importance. Here, you and I are engaged in something far more significant: single-warrior combat on behalf of our sexes. I was amply motivated.

GENE: Perhaps. But you women know limits. You observe basic rules of human decency. I do not. For example, I went into that showroom and lied my ass off.

GINA: So did I.

GENE: I said I was ready to buy a car right there, in cash, for the right price.

GINA: So did I.

GENE: I said I was a Hollywood screenwriter.

GINA: I said I was a lesbian.

GENE: *What?*

GINA: Actually, I let them infer it. I wore no makeup, a tailored suit, big lapels, tapered pants, hair back, and referred several times to my "partner."

GENE: Wouldn't it have been better to flirt with the salesman? Take advantage of one of the few weapons I didn't have?

GINA: Absolutely not. Men might like it when you flirt, but they see it as a sign of stupidity. A woman who is easy in her affections is easy in every way, including easy to take advantage of.

I was a lesbian because I wanted them to understand they were dealing with the final decision maker, that there wasn't a guy somewhere who would have to okay it. And I wanted to present an impregnable front, as it were. No personal questions. All business. I also demanded the only woman sales associate, a sweet little thing with a big engagement ring. I wanted her cowed.

I also showed up in my Mercedes and parked it out front, so they understood I was for real. It was newly washed and waxed and buffed. It looked like a Nazi staff car. I was Helga von Stupp.

GENE: Very impressive.

GINA: Worried?

GENE: No. None of that is as important as the negotiating stance. I walked in and told the salesman —a very experienced, very professional guy named Bud—that all I cared about was money. He smiled. I didn't. I said I was ethnically incapable of accepting anything less than rock-bottom wholesale. If my people feel we are getting the best possible price, I said, we buy— bing-bang!—and if we feel we are not—bing-bang!—we walk out and don't come back. It was a Jewish thing, I said.

GINA: You helped perpetuate an unfair stereotype!

GENE: I did.

GINA: You dishonored your mother and father.

GENE: And my poor deceased grandma, yes. I was going to win. I went on to tell Bud that I didn't want to hear any crap about how good the service was at his dealership, the free oil changes, the friendly staff, or anything. I didn't want coupons and chamois cloths. Money. It was about money

GINA: How did he react?

GENE: He showed me a thank-you card from a client of his. It was a photo of her and her cute-as-a-button daughter. Bud happened to mention that he had helped hook the little girl up with a good doctor, for her asthma. In short, Bud was very smooth. But I stayed on message. I said I didn't want to be his friend, I wanted to squeeze him dry. Then I told him the price I wanted and dared him to beat it.

GINA: So did I.

GENE: Mine was preposterously low, but not so low that he would just shrug and stand up.

GINA: So was mine.

GENE: How did you know just how low to go?

GINA: I researched it on the Web. I found what dealerships pay for the car—the invoice price.

GENE: So did I.

GINA: Did your guy match the price?

GENE: No, but he came close.

GINA: So did mine.

GENE: Okay, what was the final, out-the-door price that you got?

GINA: Tell me yours first.

GENE: Type it. We'll e-mail it at the same instant.

GINA: Okay.

GENE: Go.

GINA: $84,600   **GENE:** $82,503

GINA: I can't believe it.

GENE: Actually, I'm surprised. You did very well.

GINA: I just can't believe you beat me. They were so scared of me they called me back after I left, and lowered the price. They were begging.

GENE: Don't feel bad. You had no chance.

GINA: I'm just stunned.

GENE: What dealership did you go to?

GINA: Mercedes-Benz of North Haven. In Connecticut.

GENE: Small place?

GINA: Pretty small.

GENE: I went to American Service Center, in Arlington, Virginia. It wasn't absolutely the largest dealership possible, but it had the largest service department.

GINA: I thought you didn't give a crap about service.

GENE: I didn't. I gave a crap about service *departments*. Because when a dealership has a large service department, it makes most of its profits there and can afford to sell its cars cheaper, even at a loss.

GINA: I never thought of that.

GENE: Neither did I. But Warren Brown did.

GINA: Who is Warren Brown?

GENE: He writes about cars for *The Washington Post*. Warren is one of the most knowledgeable people on earth about the automobile business. I asked him for advice.

GINA: You said I couldn't ask anyone for advice!

GENE: I did not.

GINA: You absolutely did! I told you I was going to ask my husband, the car fanatic, and you specifically said I couldn't do it!

GENE: Right. I said you could not ask any *man,* because if you got a *man's* advice, it would pollute the gender experiment. If you'd thought about it, you were perfectly free to ask any *woman* who knows a lot about cars, had you been able to find one in the continental United States.

GINA: You cheated.

GENE: I most certainly did not. I stayed within the rules. A combatant is not obliged to give his adversary tips. Still, the big-dealership/small-dealership thing would not explain a $2,100 difference.

GINA: What would?

GENE: Complete ruthlessness. When I got down to real negotiation with my salesman, I told him I knew his invoice price, so I knew what his profit would be, and I wanted it low.

GINA: That's what I did! And it's the same invoice price!

GENE: Correct. So my salesman made this big show of checking with his manager.

GINA: So did mine.

GENE: And then he came back and offered me a very low price.

GINA: So did she.

GENE: And then I looked him in the eye and said, "Now, why you don't go back to your manager and get me some of the holdback."

GINA: What?

GENE: And my salesman sighed, said, "Hang on," and walked out.

GINA: What's a holdback?

GENE: In addition to the 6.2 percent markup over invoice that the salesman has to work with on a Mercedes S-Class car, there is an additional 3 percent that the dealership gets to keep in reserve. It is discretionary with them whether they will ever apply it to a purchase. Very few people know about this. Even Warren didn't mention it.

GINA: How did you find out?

GENE: I called a dealership fifty miles away and spoke to a young salesman there. I told him I was working on a book and that I needed to know the real pricing structure for a Mercedes. I told him, truthfully, that I was not buying a Mercedes and would not use anything he told me for personal financial gain. I flattered the hell out of him. He told me about the holdback.

So, anyway, Bud the salesman came back and said he got me $1,200 out of the $2,400 reserve. I looked him in the eye and said I wanted $1,700 and that if he gave me that, I would buy the car right there, with cash. He said okay.

Then I told him the truth. To avoid getting punched in the face, I whipped out a nice bottle of wine for him. He laughed. I think he liked the fact I was trying to beat a woman. We shook hands.

GINA: I cannot believe this. You accepted all sorts of outside help that was unavailable to me.

GENE: I did not. I merely thought outside the box, and you didn't.

GINA: I'm surprised they even took you seriously, driving up in that car of yours.

GENE: I parked it two blocks away and walked.

GINA:

GENE: Admit it. You were outhustled.

GINA: I can't believe they didn't see through you.

GENE: I looked good. New hazel tweed sports jacket.

GINA: Hazel tweed?

GENE: Right.

GINA: You call it "hazel tweed"?

GENE: I call it brownish. My wife calls it hazel tweed.

GINA: What color pants did you wear?

GENE: Blackish.

GINA: Charcoal?

GENE: That's what my wife called it!

GINA: And your shirt?

GENE: Sort of tan.

GINA: Very elegant combination. A little daring, even.

GENE: It looked good.

GINA: Your wife assembled it for you, didn't she?

GENE: Of course.

GINA: You accepted her advice on how to dress.

GENE: Sure.

GINA: So I was not free to consult a man, but you were free to consult a woman?

GENE:

GINA: You cheated.

GENE: It was no big deal. It only involved clothing.

GINA: Presentation was essential to the process! You cheated, totally and irredeemably! You subverted the process and the results are invalid.

GENE: I did not subvert anything.

GINA: Is your wife a woman?

GENE:

GINA: Are you not *sure* if your wife is a woman?

GENE: She is a woman.

GINA: And you not only sought her assistance but accepted it?

GENE: I probably shouldn't have.

GINA: You got that right.

GENE: At the time, I didn't think it was unfair. But I see your point.

GINA: All right, then.

GENE: I'm sorry.

GINA: It's okay.

GENE: Then we're done here?

GINA: You really, honestly, acknowledge for the record that you broke the rules and that you're sorry?

GENE: Yes. I apologize.

GINA: Okay. We're done.

GENE: Good.

GINA: We'll talk tomorrow, then?

GENE: Yep. Bye.

GINA: Bye.

GENE:

GENE: Gina? You still there?

GENE:

GENE: I guess not.

GENE:

GENE: I won.

25

Fighting Like Cats and Doggerel

GENE: We are writing this on the weekend of Valentine's Day, a holiday dating to medieval times, when medieval men and medieval women celebrated their love for each other by bathing, just this once.

GINA: You don't know anything about Valentine's Day, do you?

GENE: No.

GINA: It happens to have a very romantic past. It was named for a third-century Roman bishop who was executed for secretly officiating at marriages of young lovers against the wishes of the king. The king wanted his soldiers suitably brutal, unencumbered by soft feelings for family. In his prison cell awaiting his beheading, Bishop Valentine fell in love with the beautiful but blind daughter of his jailer, Asterius. First he cured her blindness, then on the day of his execution—February 14—wrote her a farewell note that he signed, "From your Valentine."

GENE: Awwwwwwww.

GINA: I know. It makes me all misty.

GENE: I'm sure it does. Are you bothered at all by the chokingly obvious problems of verisimilitude, beginning with the curing-her-blindness part?

GINA: Not at all.

GENE: The story was probably invented around 1953 by someone named Irving "Sappy" Sapirstein, national sales director for the floral-arrangement industry. That's just a guess.

GINA: Valentine's Day is not about literal truth. It is about idealized truth. There is nothing wrong with that.

GENE: It is also about getting expensive gifts from men, no?

GINA: There is nothing wrong with that, either.

GENE: Chicks dig gifts. This we understand.

GINA: Not all gifts. Some gifts are aggressively bad, because they convey the wrong message. Women are much better at giving gifts, because we take into account what our men ought to like but don't, which is why we buy them beautiful, paisley silk boxer shorts they never wear but should.

GENE: Women's gift giving is corrective?

GINA: I would prefer "instructive." But there is love and care behind it. It is lovingly instructive. Men tend to give gifts out of a sense of duty, putting as little thought into it as possible. Generic flowers and chocolates are not good gifts, no matter how much they cost. They are good gifts if they are your *favorite* flowers or the ones you carried in your wedding bouquet (and of course your husband memorized your wedding bouquet), or the chocolates are ones he ordered from the little place in Belgium you went to on your fifth anniversary.

GENE: I thought the message of a gift is "I love and appreciate you." Anything nice qualifies.

GINA: No. Gifts are much more complicated than that. The message is much more subtle. It must reflect a sophisticated knowledge of your woman's desires. Men need to learn this. Surprisingly, it is not impossible to teach them.

On our first Valentine's Day together, for example, my husband got me a cookbook. My reaction to this present was so dramatic that it is now indelibly etched on a certain part of his brain, the part of one's brain that retains and closets things too painful to confront: the trauma of one's own birth, the death of one's parents, the agony of a broken limb, and so forth.

Last Valentine's Day, Michael gave me gorgeous—and, coincidentally, expensive—custom-made boots. The boot maker measured my foot. I chose the leather. On the inside it says "Made exclusively for Gina Barreca." He has learned, my husband. He is a good man. An educator, and an educable man.

I have almost but not quite forgotten that cookbook, which may have been the worst present a man ever got for a woman.

GENE: It was not remotely the worst present a man ever got for a woman. My friend Pat Myers was the recipient of the worst present a man ever got for a woman. Right, Pat?

PAT: Right. Hi, Gina.

GINA: Hi. Are you the same Pat who ended your tennis game in a tie because neither you nor your girlfriend wanted to make the other one feel bad by losing?

PAT: That's me.

GINA: I like you.

PAT: Thank you!

GENE: Can I interrupt here?

PAT: I like you, too, Gina. You're funny.

GINA: Thank you!

GENE: Ladies, we're sliding off topic.

GINA: We are establishing a rapport.

PAT: I think that's important.

GENE: Swell. Okay, Pat, can you tell Gina what your husband, Mark, got you as a present on or about December 25, 1986?

PAT: He got me a bathroom scale.

GINA: **Wow!**

Gene: Kinda makes your cookbook seem like the Star of India, doesn't it?

PAT: It's like a woman buying her husband a penis pump.

GINA: Why are you still married to this individual?

PAT: Because he is also trustworthy, loyal, helpful, friendly, courteous, kind, sexy, cheerful, thrifty, brave, clean, and reverent, at least most of the time. I can deal with a little unsentimentality.

GINA: You are a saint.

GENE: So is Valentine.

PAT: Valentine?

GENE: It's the subject at hand. Valentine's Day. We've been discussing what distinguishes good presents from bad ones.

PAT: Good presents are ones that are not bathroom scales.

GINA: Pat, I love you as a new friend, but I cannot let this stand. On this front, you are like a prisoner of war, dreaming of the culinary delights offered at an IHOP. On behalf of all women worldwide, I need to lobby for a substantially higher threshold.

GENE: How much of this threshold involves capital expenditure?

GINA: None. It is entirely about thoughtfulness. Probably the best present I can imagine is an original poem.

GENE: Really?

GINA: Really.

GENE: Is that a challenge?

GINA: Yes.

From Gene, to Women

To prove that we men aren't clods
Nor romantically inept,
I offer up this Valentine
To those with whom we've slept.

Whoops, that was crasser than I meant
May no offense be taken.
(When trying to be sweet as jam,
Men sometimes sound like bacon.)

It's in tribute that I write this
To our girlfriends and our wives,
The very folks without whom
We'd live unexamined lives.

We admit we're fixer-uppers,
And we know how much you'd care
To remodel this old eyesore
Into a darling pied-à-terre.

Some things, alas, just cannot change—
We're hopeless on minutiae.
We'll never learn the differences
'Tween violet, mauve, and fuchsia.

We'll never get the hang of which
Utensil's on the right,
Or why you have to make the bed
Before getting in at night.

Or why you hate the seat left up
And lecture us, and frown.
(We never criticize *you*
When you leave the damn thing down.)

We're not good with our emotions,
However hard we try,
And we know our lack of feeling
Is enough to make you cry.

And cry and cry and cry some more,
A weeping, bawling mewlery.
Thank God we've learned the cure for this
Is nice, expensive jewelry.

The purpose of this poem
(Please ignore missteps above)
Is to make you understand that
What we feel for you is love.

It's love for all the things you are
And—I'm not sure how to put it—
For something else we would explain
If we only understood it.

We love the fact that even when
You're sweating like a sow,
You manage to smell better
Than us at rest, somehow.

We know that we are less mature
And our follies leave you seething—
Wasting time when we could achieve
Thinner thighs through tantric breathing.

You help us guard against excess
With lists of don'ts and dos.
On these you put your foot down,
In one of your 6,427 pairs of nearly identical
        but subtly different and obviously essential
        (and even sometimes custom-made)
        shoes.

You want to "bond" so much you'll watch
Our sports on TV stations—
Then plant your butts to block the screen
In third-down situations.

You think that we are louts and boors,
And condescending varmints.
But we forgive you, 'cause you wear
Those splendid undergarments.

See, we really understand you
In almost every way
Except for everything you do
And everything you say.

In short, you drive us wild with want
And also up a wall.
We wish you'd change in every way,
And also not at all.

From Gina, to Men

"Boys will be boys," they said to me from infancy to menopause,
It's true. And so, at forty-six, for real complaint I've got no cause.
They're what they are, for good and bad, from their top right to
    their bottom,
It makes for quite a tidy list, to tick off, *seriatim:*

    1. They are not mature.
    2. They are not aware.
    3. They do not emote.
    4. They do not play fair.

    5. They warm the bed.
    6. Their smiles are winning.
    7. They go to your head.
    8. They invented sinning.

9. They forgive and forget
10. (But they'd forget anyway.)
11. They'll remember sports scores
12. But not your birthday.

13. They like competition.
14. They don't like to lose.
15. They prefer certain women
16. (But don't make them choose.)

17. Even when they are wrong
18. They think they are right.
19. They're of limited use
20. Though they will drive at night.

21. One day they'll grill chicken
22. And then call us to look
23. At their wondrous creation:
24. "I'm such a great cook!"

25. They don't like to discuss it.
26. It's conflict they fear.
27. But they'll fight to the death
28. Over one can of beer.

29. Although they'll feel bad
30. If they damage a fender,
31. They'll blithely hurt feelings—
32. They're the untender gender.

33. They'll waltz into your world
34. And make your heart melt
35. Then split in a heartbeat
36. Leaving socks and a belt.

37. Men are complex
38. Both shallow and deep;
39. Too often disguising
40. The wolf in the sheep.

41. And yet we adore them.
42. What else can we do?
43. Love them or leave them,
44. They infect you like flu.

45. Plus, the sex isn't bad
46. If they factor in you.

THE FINAL CHAPTER

Until We Meet A~~gain~~

GENE: Here we are.

GINA: Hard to believe.

GENE: Homestretch. Two-minute warning. Bottom of the ninth. Final chukker.

GINA:

GENE: Negatory on the sports metaphors?

GINA: Correct.

GENE: No problem. I'm in a good mood. I've figured something out.

GINA: What?

GENE: I think you were right, back there at the beginning. I think we need to meet.

GINA: *What?*

GENE: I think we should stop right here, travel to neutral territory, and meet for lunch. New York. My treat. Then we come back and write about it.

GINA: Why?

GENE: It'll deliver a sense of closure.

GINA: The publisher was pretty clear he didn't want us to. I don't want to tick him off.

GENE: I just talked to him. He said it's okay with him if we feel it's better for the book.

GINA: You're kidding.

GENE: Nope. So, when are you free?

GINA: I'm pretty busy the next few weeks.

GENE: There's no rush.

GINA:

GENE: What?

GINA: I changed my mind.

GENE: About what?

GINA: I'm feeling comfortable with our relationship the way it is.

GENE: We don't *have* a "relationship." We're pen pals!

GINA: Pen pals?

GENE: In a sense.

GINA: Is that all this has meant to you?

GENE:

GINA: What?

GENE: I'm trying to figure out what's going on here.

GINA: What's going on here is that you are exhibiting all the self-awareness and sensitivity for which your sex is famous. *Pen pals?* We know each other better than a lot of married couples know each other.

GENE: That's true. We've got a good thing going. So, why not meet?

GINA: Why risk ruining it?

GENE: *Ruining* it?

GINA: That could happen if we met.

GENE: Gina?

GINA: What?

GENE: You're talking as though we have a romantic relationship.

GINA: We do.

GENE: We *do?*

GINA: It *is* a romantic relationship. It's not a sexual relationship, but it's a romantic relationship. Are you denying it is a romantic relationship? What am I to you?

GENE: Are you kidding? The reader has a right to know if you are kidding.

GINA: I'm completely serious.

GENE: This is not a shtick?

GINA: This is not a shtick. What have we been doing for two years but an extended, elaborate flirtation? While we've been arguing with each other and making fun of each other, haven't we been sharing real anxieties? And secrets? Didn't you tell me about that thing you did to someone a long time ago that you still have nightmares about?

GENE: We didn't write about that.

GINA: My point exactly. Just how much of a hammerhead are you? How is this not an intimate relationship?

GENE: Okay. Point conceded.

GINA: Thank you.

GENE: So, let's do lunch.

GINA: No.

GENE: Why?

GINA: I just don't think it would be a good idea.

GENE:

GINA: What?

GENE: You're afraid.

GINA: No, I am not "afraid."

GENE: Then why?

GINA: It's not right for the dynamic of the book. I think a little lingering mystery is good.

GENE: So, let's get this straight. You think, one, this is a romantic relationship and, two, a little lingering mystery is good.

GINA: Yes.

GENE: Do you ever give advice to girlfriends who are going through crises of the heart?

GINA: Only several dozen times a week.

GENE: So, let's say a girlfriend—we'll call her, oh, I don't know, Shmina Shmarreca—came to you with a certain problem. Let's say she was crazy about this guy—

GINA: I am not crazy about you.

GENE: She really *liked* this guy she never met. They only talked on the phone, and wrote letters to each other, and she found him smart and funny and sweet.

GINA: I never said I found you "sweet."

GENE: Smart and funny and Jewish. And she wondered what she should do about this, not because she wanted to have a physical relationship with him, but because she sort of wanted to get to know him better, because it seemed like a natural thing to do. You of course would advise Shmina to FOR GOD'S SAKE NEVER MEET THE GUY BECAUSE EYE CONTACT IS A TERRIBLE THING, THAT ACTUAL COMMUNICATION IS SOMETHING TO BE AVOIDED BY HUMAN PEOPLE AT ALL COSTS.

Right?

GINA: You are so totally, reprehensibly twisting the situation.

GENE: Untwist it, then.

GINA: My point is that we have a sort of idealized view of each other. It's a romantic relationship, but an entirely intellectualized one. You have become everyman to me, and I have become everywoman to you. It's worked, for the book. It's allowed us to examine intimate things from an almost scientific standpoint, without the sorts of complications that arise when a man and a woman also relate physically. It's given a validity to our discussions. I'm making a purely professional argument here, about what's best for the book.

GENE: Valid point. One problem.

GINA: What?

GENE: The book is done.

GINA: Well, yes.

GENE: Now maybe we can learn something—*for the book*— about how actually having to physically relate to each other might affect the way we deal with each other. It could be an important insight into the male-female dynamic. I am making a purely professional argument here, about what's best *for the book*.

GINA:

GENE:

GINA: Why should we become like other people?

GENE: What?

GINA: We have a special relationship, unlike any relationship I've ever had or even heard about. Once we meet, it'll dwindle into a mere run-of-the-mill friendship.

GENE: Well, we're going to be meeting eventually, when the book comes out. We have to give interviews together.

GINA: I know.

GENE: So, what's the big deal?

GINA: It just doesn't feel like it's the right time.

GENE:

GINA: Later is better.

GENE:

GINA:

GENE: You're afraid.

GINA: Maybe a little.

GENE: Whoa.

GINA: Are you going to be nasty now?

GENE: No.

GINA: Thank you.

GENE: What are you afraid of?

GINA: I'm afraid we might disappoint each other.

GENE: It's possible that I might disappoint you. I'm sort of shleppy-looking. But I know you won't disappoint me.

GINA: See, just *saying* that I won't disappoint you means you have an expectation of not being disappointed, which means the likelihood of your being disappointed is *hugely* greater than if you expected to be disappointed. Before, I was wavering. Now, I'm absolutely certain. We can't meet.

GENE: *How am I supposed to react to that?*

GINA: It is immaterial how you react, because the matter is closed. You've shown a contemptible bias that irreparably skews the equation.

GENE: What equation?

GINA: The equation of your disappointment level plotted against your expectational curve.

GENE: My expectational curve?

GINA: You know what I mean. If you want to make me sound foolish, go right ahead.

GENE: I don't want to make you sound foolish.

GINA:

GENE: I like you.

GINA:

GENE:

GINA: Well, I like you, too.

GENE: I'm not sure why we're having a problem here. You're not afraid that something will . . . *happen,* right?

GINA: You mean, like . . .

GENE: Right.

GINA: No. That's not it.

GENE: Well?

GINA: Well, there are just no guidelines for this sort of thing. There's no template. Usually if a man and a woman have a flirtatious relationship, an intense emotional relationship of some sort, whether sexual or not, they conduct it from the very start in each other's physical presence. That means that their physical persons—not just their looks, but their demeanor, their habits, and whatnot—are a given. They were weighed and analyzed prior to the development of the relationship. If they were incompatible, the relationship never developed. If they were not incompatible, these physical things were kneaded right into the relationship. They could not suddenly arise as a surprise or a disappointment. I'm just as afraid that you'll disappoint me as I am that I'll disappoint you.

GENE: But why should that bother you if nothing comes of this but a business partnership? So what if we're a little disappointed in the reality?

GINA: Because it's so good the way it is.

GENE:

GINA:

GENE:

GINA: I'm afraid you'll think I'm fat.

GENE: Ah.

GINA: I am not fat. I am "average." And we know what *that* means, thanks to your gleefully calling up a coroner to find out the weight of a corpse. I weigh more than a dead Marilyn, but because size is something you notice, and your own wife is a little teeny morsel, and you talk gaga about her all the time, I feel I will *loom large* over the table when we meet for lunch, like a Macy's Thanksgiving Day Parade float.

GENE: I'm "average," too.

GINA: Are you very short?

GENE: No.

GINA: Really crummy teeth?

GENE: No.

GINA: Well, then it's no good. There is no parity. It's not fair, but that's the way it is.

GENE: Would it be indelicate of me to point out that your position is not entirely consistent with contemporary feminist theory?

GINA: Yes, it would be. It would also not be entirely accurate. Contemporary feminists are neither delusional or dishonest. We understand that there are emotional inequities between the sexes, and we do not think it dreadful or shameful that—in return for the hundreds of advantages nature has given us—women are burdened by a disproportionate need to be loved.

GENE: Loved?

GINA: Loved.

GENE:

GINA: Because that's what it comes down to. So we worry

inordinately—and, at our worst, neurotically—about our physical appearance and how we will be perceived. And there is nothing we can do about it. It doesn't help that men are shallow and judge us in simplistic ways. It doesn't help that men are congenitally blind to what is inside another person.

GENE: I see.

GINA: That's just the way it is.

GENE: Before we first spoke, I expected you to be a jerk. Actually, I brought a *double* prejudice to our first conversation, because you were both an academic—which meant, to me, an ass-wipe—and a professional feminist, which meant, to me, someone poisoned by an angry ideology that exterminates both a sense of humor and a sense of proportion. Well, it turned out you were neither of those things. You were a hoot. The realization actually caused me to reexamine some of my assumptions. It civilized me a little.

There is no pretense to you, not a hint of stuffiness or elitism. One of your closest friends happens to be the woman who cleans your house. I've never known anyone else with as much self-assurance and as little self-importance.

I've also never known anyone so opinionated and so aggressive who is also so sensitive to the opinions of others. You aren't thin-skinned, you're tender. You make a grand show of being tough, but when an idiot letter writer took exception to something you said in my column and called you a "bitch," you weren't angry. You were hurt.

As a bitch, you're a fraud.

In two years of writing together, I've never seen you hesitate to admit to some behavior or some attitude that you knew would make you look weak or silly or inconsistent. You are comfortable with who you are—unapologetically, ruefully, joyfully yourself. That sort of thing is infectious. You must be a terrific teacher.

That's one part of you. Another part is still twelve years old, staring at that schnauzer-sized condom filled with water, half scared and half thrilled. That's a good part, too.

Above all, you're a 220-volt appliance in a world wired for 110. Sparks fly. When I answer the phone and hear, "It's Gina!" this is what it sounds like: "It's *show* time!" And it is—a three-ring affair with monkeys and zebras and contortionists and cotton candy in disturbing but interesting pastels. You're fun.

GINA:

GENE:

GINA: You bastard.

GENE: Heh heh heh.

GINA:

GENE: So, do we meet?

GINA: *Definitely* not.

GENE: Okay. When the book comes out.

GINA: Right.

GENE: Good.

GINA: Now I'm nervous.

GENE: I'm not.

GINA:

GENE:

GINA: I don't think I like the way this is ending.

GENE: I do.

Made in the USA
Middletown, DE
21 November 2014